In The Wake Of The Sword

Originally published In 1917 by Erskine Macdonald Ltd, London

& Collected Poems

Printed in various publications between 1914 and 1930

An annotated and illustrated 2023 reprint with new introduction by Lucy London, additional biographical details, appendices and illustrations.

Edited by Paul Breeze

Interesting Books...
...Fascinating Subjects!

POSH UP NORTH
Publishing

www.poshupnorth.com

Publishing History

"In The Wake Of The Sword" was originally published In 1917 by Erskine
MacDonald Ltd , London.

The other poems reproduced were first published as indicated.

This edition reprinted in 2023 as a centenary reissue, revised and expanded
edition with a new foreword,introduction, a number of new photographs and
illustrations, new additional back pages by Posh Up North Publishing, New
Brighton

ISBN: 978-1-909643-55-0

Concept and introduction by Lucy London
Biography and additional research by Paul Breeze

CONTENTS

Collected Poems From Magazines and Journals 64

Reviews And Other Press Cuttings 106

Foreword: A Tale of Two Percys.

When you are doing historical research, you rely a lot on the various records and archives that are available and that the information that is recorded in them is correct.

There are often queries about spellings and dates but you can usually get around them by referring to corroborating evidence taken from other sources - and a bit of educated guess work.

Obviously, if the person that you are researching had an unusual name like "Marmaduke Hossenpfeffer", they will be a lot easier to track down on the various Births, Marriages and Deaths registers, electoral rolls and census records than trying to work out which of the thousands upon thousands of John Smiths might be the one that you are looking for.

So when it came to gen-ning up on a poet called Percy Haselden who wrote about the Mersey, the fact that a soldier called Percy Haselden from Liverpool was killed at the Somme seemed to fit the bill. After all, how many Percy Haseldens could there possibly be on Merseyside...?

We thus included Percy in our Somme Poets book - and our Merseyside Poets book - and in various exhibitions that we produced and staged over the period of the Great War centenary years.

All well and good – but now let's fast forward to early 2023 when we were contacted by Linda Michelini who informed us that there were actually TWO SEPARATE Percy Haseldens.

Linda had been researching the history of the Liverpool Pals Regiment in the First World War and was well aware of the Somme Percy Haselden. However, through her own researches, she was able to establish that the guy who had written the poem "Searchlights On The Mersey" – and, indeed, lots of other poems as well – wasn't the same Percy Haselden at all.

Now, having long gone along with the conclusion that the poet Percy Haselden had been lost without trace in 1916, we admittedly didn't really put much effort into looking into him after that. Well – you wouldn't, would you?

Take the case of the more well-known WW1 soldier poet Wilfred Owen. His short life and unfortunate death on the banks of the Ours canal just a week before the Armistice have all been well documented and picked to bits over the years and, having firmly established that he died in 1918, I doubt that very many people have ever put an awful lot of effort into trying to find out what he did after the war...

After all, it's not as if he did an "Elvis" who, according to certain conspiracy theorists over the years, got fed up with being in the limelight and went off to live in seclusion on a tropical island somewhere. Or Adolf Hiter escaping to Paraguay at the end of WW2 and still living happily in the South American rainforest at the ripe old age of 134 – or Princess Diana and Dodi el Fayed sneaking off to live a quiet life undisturbed by the Paparazzi...

And it's the same with Percy Haselden. As he was reported missing, believed dead, on the Somme in 1916, and – despite a wide reaching media campaign at the time - his mother never heard of him again, there's very little mileage for us as researchers to investigate the likelihood that he did anything else in the post war years.

But thanks to the information uncovered by Linda, it turns out that the poet Percy Haselden was actually born Percy EVANS, that Haselden was his mother's maiden name - and his middle name - and that he used the name Percy Haselden for all his writing, which is the root of all the confusion.

So, armed with these new facts, we had a concerted look into Percy Haselden Evans and found out all sorts of fascinating things about him and his family.

They lived on the Wirral – which is where we now live – and, for much of that time, they actually lived just down the road from us, which is an amazing coincidence!

We discovered that - unlike his unfortunate Somme namesake - Percy Haselden Evans went on to have a long and varied life, got married, started a family and lived until 1959.

He had numerous poems published in all sorts of magazines and journals over the years – during and after the First World War - and the fruits of our updated research are what you can now see in the following pages.

There is a lot that we still don't know – but here is what we do know…

Paul Breeze,

Editor & Publisher

Introduction to the 2023 Edition by Lucy London

I began my commemorative exhibition project by researching women who wrote poetry during the First World War. I wanted to tell people about the war, so I later extended my scope to also include male poets, writers and artsts from as many countries as possible for this was the first conflict that affected every country in the world.

In 2014 Historian Debbie Cameron contacted me to tell me about Percy Haselden, a WW1 soldier poet she had discovered.

I checked in my copy of Catherine W. Reilly's wonderful "English Poets of the First World War: A Bibliography" (St. Martin's Press, New York, 1978) and found on pages 7, 31 and 162, information that tells us Percy Haselden's war poems were published by Erskine Macdonald, London in 1917 under the title "In the wake of the Sword".

His poem "Searchlights on the Mersey" was published in "The Fiery Cross: an Anthology" edited by Mabel C. Edwards and Mary Booth and published by Grant Richards in 1915 and that he had a poem published in the WW1 Anthology "The Great War in Verse and Prose" edited by James Elgin Wetherell, (Legislative Assembly of Ontario, Toronto, Printed and Published by A. T. WILGRESS, 1919.)

In April 2023, Linda Woodfine Michelini contacted me to say that the information on my Fascinating Facts of the Great War weblog in 2014 (i.e. before I began researching

WW1 male poets properly in 2016) about the poet Percy Haselden was incorrect.

Linda says: " I discovered the poet known as Percy Haselden was in fact born Percy Haselden Evans when I googled his name, trying to find out as much as I could to verify information for my Liverpool Pals bio. I also came across a mention of Percy in the Denstone School Magazine "The Denstonian", which decided it - he wasn't the Percy Haselden I was looking for."

Linda tells us that Percy was educated at Denstone College in Staffordshire and, according to Denstone College Magazine, Percy wrote using the name Percy Haselden. As there are quite a few Percy Haseldens listed on Find my Past and other websites, it became quite difficult to find exact information.

Lucy London, May 2023

Acknowledgements:

My thanks are due to

Historian Debbie Cameron who has commemorative First World War Facebook Groups and weblogs and who has supported my commemorative project since it began in 2012. Links to Debbie's research:

https://historicalclues.blogspot.com/

Remembering British women In WW1 -The Home Front & Overseas
(Facebook Group https://www.facebook.com/groups/1468972083412699)

Stories of Women of The First World War Brooch.
(Facebook Group   https://www.facebook.com/groups/1767775906637896)

Dr Margaret Stetz, Mae and Robert Carter Professor of Women's Studies and Professor of Humanities at the University of Delaware in America, for her help and support with my commemorative project.

Linda Woodfine Michelini, who contacted me to tell me my initial post in 2014 about Percy Haselden was incorrect, and gave me valuable information that led to finding out more about Percy. Linda is one of the researchers for the Liverpool Pals in the First World War.

To find out more about the Liverpool Pals, please visit their website http://liverpoolpals.com

And as always to Paul Breeze for his outstanding research and publishing skills and for writing up the history of the Haselden Evans family.

Percy Haselden Family Background and Brief Biography

Percy Haselden Evans was born on 5th December 1886, in Liscard, Wirral, UK.

His family name was actually Evans coming from his father William Parry Evans (1845 – 1922) a Cotton Broker originally from Liverpool - and the Haselden was a middle name that came from his mother's family name – Matilda Haselden (1857-1939)

He had 7 siblings:

Julia Dorothy Evans (1889 – 1963)

Matilda Evans (born 1889)

William Laurence Evans (1892-1954)

Esther Josephine Evans (1894-1959)

Ruth Haselden Evans (1896-1984)

Lily Haselden Evans (born 1897)

Doris Haselden Evans (1900-1965)

Background to the Haseldens.

Percy's mother Matilda Haselden was born on 14th September 1857 and was baptised as a Catholic at St Albans Catholic Church in Wallasey on 4th October 1857.

Her parents were William Henry Haselden (born in Liverpool in 1824) and Margaret nee Kehoe, (born Ireland, 1830). They married in Waterford, Ireland on 14th December 1845.

They all lived with her grandfather – William Haselden – born in 1794 (birth place not specified), grandmother Elizabeth (born Cumberland 1799) three siblings Edward Joseph (born 1848), Elizabeth (1847) and Edith (1856) and 2 live-in servants.

At the time of the 1851 and 1861 censuses, the Haselden family lived at Oak Dale Cottage, Wheatland Lane, Poulton cum Seacombe, Birkenhead, Cheshire, England.

William (grandfather) was a Shipbuilder & government lawyer of emigration ships at the port of Liverpool and William Henry started off as a shipwright but later became an inspector of Emigration Ships.

Matilda's father William Henry died, age 38, on 2nd October 1863 at the Guildhall Hotel, Cheapside in London. Probate was granted to his widow Margaret Philomena Haselden.

By 1871, the remaining Haselden family had moved to Sefton Villa, Belgrave Street in Liscard. We don't know what happened to the mother as she doesn't appear on any more census returns and, by then, the household comprised only of William (grandfather) and Edward, Elizabeth and Matilda (age 13).

Grandfather William died on 25th August 1873 age 81 (Liverpool Mercury 26th Aug 1873).

On the 1881 census, Edward and Elizabeth and are shown as living on Belgrave Street in Liscard and both are employed in "dividends and houses".

The head of the household is now shown as Margaret Miller, a 52 year old widow originally born in Ireland and her son – Percy A Miller – an 11 year old student born in Liverpool. Margaret's occupation here is described as "dividends and annuity".

Elizabeth and Edward are described here as the "son" and "daughter" of the household which, in terms of Margaret Miller is not entirely true but may suggest that she was a some sort of latter day carer / companion of their grandfather William prior to his death in 1873. It would also explain why Percy Miller is referred to as a "brother in law" in later documents.

This relationship between the Miller and Haselden families in quite interesting. Percy Miller is shown on the 1871 Census living with both his parents on Belvidere Road, Toxteth Park, Liverpool – father Alexander Miller, a retired builder - born 1814 Lancashire, and mother Margaret born 1829 Ireland. The family must have been quite well off as they had 3 servants.

Somewhat mysteriously there is also mention of a "step daughter" called Edith Haselden born Cheshire 1856. Edith does not appear with the rest of the Haselden family on the 1871 Census and it is not really clear why she would be living with the Millers at that time and being referred to as a step daughter.

Edith married William Gate in 1878 at St Hilary's Church in Wallasey when she was 22. William was 36 and a widower with 4 children from his first wife Isabel who died in 1874.

3 of those children died in infancy but William and Edith went on to have 8 more children together – 7 girls and 1 boy - so it must have been a happy, if rather full, household!

Elizabeth Haselden married John Davies at New Brighton in 1885 - when she was 38 years old - and they had a daughter Elizabeth, born in 1887.

John Davies must have died because, by 1901, Elizabeth was a widow living with the daughter at 2 Meadow Street,

Ball Avenue, Liscard. Also part of the household was her still unmarried brother Edward Joseph. Both siblings were still "living by their own means".

William Haselden Gate (Percy's Cousin)

Edith's only son, William Haselden Gate, was listed as an electrical engineer on the 1901 census living at the family home at Holland Road in Liscard and he must have, at some point, gone to work in Africa as he married a South African girl called Millicent Wolseley Stuart in Lourenco Marques in Mozambique prior to WW1.

Millicent's family background is rather interesting and worthy of a few lines here – even though it has nothing whatsoever to do with Percy.

Her father James Townson Stuart – who, oddly enough, happens to be the only member of the whole Haselden Evans extended family that we actually have a photo of - had been born in Kingston, Jamaica, in 1842. According to Jamaican records, in his youth he married a domestic free slave (whatever that means...) and worked as a clerk on the Jamaica National Railway.

We don't know what happened to the wife and the next thing we know about James is that he ended up living in Durban, Natal Province (South Africa), and working as a Post Office clerk

It was there around August 1865 that he married Elizabeth Mary Towning - who was English born to English parents who had emigrated to Natal – and they went on to have 9 children between 1865 and 1885, of whom Millicent was the youngest.

We have no idea how William and Millicent came to meet, or why they got married in Mozambique, but it would be interesting to learn more. It would appear that they settled in Durban and had 2 children, although we know nothing about them

What we do know is that William enlisted in the South African army on 31st August 1917 and became mechanician sergeant MT-7117 in the S. African Service Corps (MT).

According to a post on the Great War Forum, he arrived at Kilwa on the coast of Tanganyika – then German East Africa - on 25th October and was assigned to the Rail Tractor Repair Company on 13th November. He was injured on 11th December when a tractor he was riding on was accidentally derailed, was moved to the 2nd SA General Hospital at Dar-es-Salaam where he died 3 days later of a fractured spine, aged 32.

William Haselden Gate is buried Dar-es-Salaam War Cemetery in modern day Tanzania, Grave Ref. 4.A.2. He also appears on the war memorial at Rhosneigr in North Wales near where his mother Edith was living in Prestatyn.

Evans Family Background

Percy's father – William Parry Evans – was born on 6th March 1845 in West Derby (Liverpool).

His parents were William Evans – and chemist and druggists, born in, Denbighshire, Wales in 1815 and Anne nee Parry who was also born in Denbighshire in 1815.

By the time of the 1851 census, The Evans family were living on Islington in Liverpool and had 4 children:

Sarah Evans - born 1843

William Parry Evans - born 1845

Mary Grace Evans – born 1847

And Edward G Evans - born 1849

A further sister - Elizabeth - came along in 1853

There seems to been a series of tragedies that hit the Evans family as the mother Anne, daughter Mary Grace and son Edward G all seem to have died in the mid 1850s and, by the time of the 1861 census, the remaining family - William Snr (now a widower), Sarah, William Parry and Elizabeth - were living at 11, Plumpton Street, Everton, West Derby, Lancashire, England.

We can't find the Evans family on the 1871 Census, which is very frustrating as we lose track of most of them after that – there being too many Evans around to be able to work out which might be ours.

By the time of the 1881 Census, William Parry Evans was listed as boarding on the opposite side of the River Mersey with the Langtrey family on Rice Hey Road in Liscard.

He was aged 36 and working as a cotton broker. He married Matilda Haselden on 12th August 1884 at St Hilary's Church in Wallasey.

The "Haselden Evans" Family

On the 1891 Census, William Parry Evans and his wife Matilda nee Haselden were living at Woodleigh, Mount Pleasant Road, Liscard. Listed at the time were William and Matilda with children Percy and Matilda.

There was also a "brother in law" listed called Percy A Miller (who we have mentioned already...), a 21 year old Oxford student born in Liverpool.

The household also had 3 live in servants: Margaret Fellowes a 26yr old domestic housemaid from Seacombe, Elizabeth Martin a 45 year old nursemaid from Birkenhead and Elizabeth McCullock, a 58 year old cook domestic from Scotland.

On the 1901 Census, the Evans family were living at 7 Belgrave Street in Liscard. They had a visitor called Elizabeth S Wakefield - 80 years old from Liverpool - and 2 servants: Statia Kiely – a 31 year old cook domestic from Ireland and Annie Barton a 24 year old nursemaid from Liverpool.

End Cliff

On the 1911 Census, the Evans family were living at End Cliff on Wellington Road in New Brighton. William and Matilda were listed as residents, along with children Percy, (art master), Julia, William (cotton brokers apprentice), Esther, Ruth, Lily and Doris.

Endcliffe, the ornate villa where the Evans family lived around 1911 in New Brighton is now a listed building converted into 6 flats. (photo by Tony Franks Buckley, Wallasey Days Gone By)

There were 2 servants – Janie Morris, an 18 year old cook domestic from Wrexham, and Mary Driver – a 19 year old household domestic, also from Wrexham.

On the 1911 and 1912 Electoral Rolls, Percy is listed as a "boarder" at his father's house at Endcliffe on Wellington Road with sole use of a second floor bedroom and part use of ground floor sitting room, furnished.

According to our friends at the fascinating "Wallasey Days Gone By" Facebook page, Endcliff, situated on Wellington Road had a tunnel leading from the cellar to the sea shore shore.

According to a story by Tom Slemen in the Liverpool Echo in 2005, the cellar, which was flooded from 6 to 11 feet due to this tunnel, was for many years the home to a sea creature -- apparently some kind of octopus -- popularly known as "Higgledy" which came and went when the tide allowed, and had been the pet of the owner around the turn of the nineteenth century; an eccentric man who is said to have fed the creature rats, chickens, and eventually his own dog.

It went on to terrorise later inhabitants, including William Parry Evans, a cotton broker, who is said to have shot at Higgledy – described as a huge black octopus with a massive beak and dead, staring eyes -- with his revolver, although he failed to kill it. Rumours as late as the 1950s said that the creature still haunted the cellar.

On the 1914 and 1915 Electoral Rolls, Percy and William are both listed as boarders at the family home Carrick (or "Carrig"...) on Victoria Road, New Brighton, each with sole use of a second floor bedroom and part use of ground floor sitting room, furnished, at a rent of £30 per annum.

William Laurence Evan (Percy's Brother)

Percy's brother William was born on 6th October 1891, trained as cotton broker and worked in his father's business.

He must have served in the First World War as he is listed as retired Major on the 1939 census but we have no record of what he did.

At the time of the 1921 Census, William is shown as living at Carrig on Victoria Road New Brighton with his parents William snr & Matilda and his daughter Margot.

In 1926, William married Eliza Doris Jackson (born Oswestry, Shropshire, 9th September 1896) in Birkenhead.

She was a career nurse and on the 1927 Electoral Roll is listed as working at the Liverpool Open Air Hospital in Leasowe, having previously worked at the Chester Royal Infirmary (1921 Census).

They had child Anthony Meredith Evans born 1929.

On the 1939 Census they lived at Hough Green, Chester. She was listed as a civil nursing reserve, William a cotton broker and retired major.

William rejoined the army in 1940 and according to the London Gazette of 6th September was appointed as an officer to the Auxiliary Military Pioneer Corps

He remained on the Army's General List after the war and left on 22nd March 1950, when he was granted the honorary rank of major (London Gazette 1950).

William died in 1954. His son Anthony went on to be a highly successful university professor.

A bit of a mystery: In 1915 William married Marjorie Wynne in Wrexham. They had a daughter Margot (she was born in Yorkshire for some reason...). We don't know what happened to Marjorie .

We know very little about William's daughter Margot other than the fact that she was born on 24th Dec 1916 and appears on the 1921 census as living with the Evans family in New Brighton.

She does not appear on the 1939 Census anywhere that we can find and in December 1945 she legally changed her name from Margot Haselden Evans to Margot Haselden White. The change was registered at the Central Office of the Supreme Court of Judicature on 15th April 1946 and subsequently reported in the London Gazette. At the time, Margot was a "spinster" and lived at 14 The Avenue, Surbiton, Surrey.

Margot Haselden White died in Weston Super Mare in 1994.

Percy Haselden Timeline

Percy Haselden Evans was born on 5ᵗʰ December 1886, in Liscard and was christened on 27ᵗʰ March 1887 at St Mary's in Liscard.

He attended Denstone College, which was a boys' private boarding school at Denstone, near Uttoxeter in Staffordshire and while we don't have his complete dates from the school- he is listed under "May '01" in the book – we presume that he stayed there until he was 18 in 1904.

He then went on to study at the Liverpool School of Art on Hope Street and began working as a part time Art Master at Wallasey Grammar School in 1909.

From 1913 to 1920 – presumably after he had finished his art studies, he became a full time art master at Wallasey Grammar School on Withens Lane in Liscard.

His entry in the The Denstone Register 1879-1930 – a directory of school alumni – back this us with its reference:

> Haselden, Percy Haselden (late Evans PH). 32 Warley Mount, Brentwood, Essex. iv. – Div. (July '03); HMH Liverpool School of Art '04-'12; National Award '11; Art Master Wallasey Grammar School '09-'20; Brentwood School since '20

> Published In The Wake of the Sword (Macdonald) '17 Contributor to Punch, Country Life, Sunday Times, Outlook etc and included in the following Anthologies : Poems From Punch (Macmillan) '21, Child Poems from Punch (Saville) '26, The Fiery Cross (Grant Richards) '16. Exhibited at Liverpool and Southport exhibitions.

The Schoolmasters' Yearbook & Educational Directory 1915 (Year Book Press, 1915) also confirms this with its entry:

Haselden-Evans, Percy   Art Master Wallasey Grammar School.

Educ: Denstone College

5 yrs training Liverpool Sch of Art

Nat Award 1911

Exp(erience): Wallasey Grammar School since 1909

According to the Teachers Registration Council in 1920:

Percy had taught as Art Master at Wallasey Grammar School part time from 1909-1913, full time from 1913 to 1920 and was working at Sir Anthony Browne's School in Brentwood, Essex, from 1920 onwards.

He apparently had Board of Education Certificates in Antique and Still Life Painting, Anatomy, Design and Etching, Life Painting and Drawing and a National Book Prize for Life Drawing.

1921: Percy married Rose Phyllis Sutcliffe at Billericay in Essex in May 1921

The Sutcliffes came from Southport in Lancashire and Rose's father was a bank manager. There is no obvious clue as to how she and Percy met or how they came to be getting married in Essex.

1921: On the 1921 census, Percy and Rose were boarders with the Hudson family at 217 Ongar Road, Brentwood in Essex. Percy was listed as at art master in Brentford.

1922: Percy's father William Parry Evans died on 29th August 1922 at his home Carrig on Victoria Road, age 77. He had retired from active business life the year before and had completed nearly 60 years in the cotton trade. (Liverpool Echo 30th Aug 1922)

1929: In August 1929 Percy – by now living at 32 Warley Mount, Brentwood - legally changed his name by Deed Poll from Percy Haselden Evans to Percy Haselden Haselden. This change of name was registered at the Central Office of the Supreme Court of Judicature on 21st August 1929. (London Gazette).

The Electoral Rolls of 1928,1929 and 1930 all show Percy and Rose living at that address and they continued to live at Warley Mount throughout the 1930s (Electoral Rolls).

1939: Percy's mother Matilda died on 11th March 1939 at the family home "Carrig". Her funeral was held at nearby St. Jame's Church on 14th March and she was buried in Wallasey Cemetery (Liverpool Daily Post, 14th March 1939).

1939: Matilda left an estate of £3,941 (Liverpool Evening Express 1st July 1939).

1939 Census

The 1939 Census shows Percy (incorrectly spelt Heselden...) still living at 32 Warley Mount in Brentwood and he is described as an assistant school master (art master) travelling.

Rose and Roger (aged 2) are shown as living in Stokenham, a picturesque village near the Devon coast, along with a closed record. Rose's sister Katherine – rather gradiosely named Katherine Lord Marykin Sutcliffe - is also there, along with a 14 year old schoolboy called Peter JL Sutcliffe who must also be a relation.

We believe that Jenifer (aged 11) was away at school in Suffolk boarding with a family called Staff – but she might well be the closed record. (She is never mentioned again – anywhere...)

1940: Landmark Court Case

Following Matilda's death, an interesting legal situation arose concerning her daughter Doris Haselden Edwards as she then was, who had married John Dennis Edwards, who was a Roman Catholic, at Rathdown, Dublin, Ireland in 1920. Doris was herself baptised as a catholic on 14th May 1922 while her father was still alive.

According to William Parry Evans' Will – which had been written in 1906 – upon his death, his Estate was to be held in Trust with an income being paid to his wife for the rest of her life and the Capital and assets being subsequently left in equal shares to his 7 children upon each attaining their 21st birthday, with provisions for later grandchildren and contingencies for the residue in the case of childless deaths.

But there was a specific clause which stated that any child of his family who converted to Roman Catholicism – or any subsequent grandchild – would not be allowed to inherit any part of his estate.

The original executors of the 1906 Will and Trustees of the Estate were William's wife Matilda, Wirral based vicar Rev

Percy Alexander Miller (him again...) and the eldest son Percy Haselden Evans. However, at the time of the 1940 court case, Norman Sinclair Hewitt (1892-1983) was Trustee of the Evans will and estate.

Hewitt was a doctor and had married William's daughter Ruth Haselden Evans in Chepstow in 1920. A Royal Navy medic in the First World War, he was a GP at Stow in the Wold in Gloucestershire in the early 1920s, practised in York for a long time and in 1946 moved to Sark in the Channel Islands to take over as medical officer after the German occupation forces had left. (The Suttonian 1983 – Sutton Valene School Magazine.)

From what went on, it would appear that he insisted in sticking to the letter of the 1906 Will regarding Catholics and had withheld Doris's share of the family fortune.

This decision was challenged in a case at the Chancery Division of the High Court in London in where Mr Justice Farwell decided that Doris "had not forfeited her right to a share of income from the residuary estate and that "the will did not operate so as to cause a forfeiture for a conversion to the Catholic religion which took place before the testator died."

The declaration also covered the grandchild – Josephine Mary Edwards, born 1921 in Ireland and baptised a Catholic upon birth. (Irish Independent - Friday 19 April 1940)

The case "Re Evans - Hewitt v Edwards (1940)" set a precedent which was referred to regularly in later litigations regarding religious intolerance in inheritance issues.

1959:

Percy died on 5th July 1959 at Christchurch in Dorset. Prior to his death, Percy had previously lived at Hyde Common, Fordingbridge, Hampshire (Percy's Will).

He bequeathed his share of the Evans family estate Trust to his son Roger. There is no mention of supposed daughter Jenifer in his will.

1987: Percy's wife Rose lived on for another 28 years after her husband's death. She died on 21st January 1987 and was, at the time, living at a retirement home called Barnhaven near Tiverton in Devon.

Percy and Rose's son Roger Dominic Justin Haselden lived in Devon. He married Hilary Pallant in Suffolk in 1968 and they had a son called Andrew Geraint Haselden, born in Ipswich in 1970.

Roger then married Elizabeth Edwards in Exeter in 1976. They had two children – Kathleen Sarah Haselden (born Exeter 1977) and William Bowden Haselden (born Exeter 1979). Roger died in Chulmleigh in Devon in 2007.

Percy Haselden In the Great War

Having firmly established that that Percy Haselden Evans the poet did NOT die in the Somme 1916, we figured that we ought to try and find out what he DID do during the First World War.

Despite there being a huge amount of resources available for checking that sort of thing nowadays, we still had a lot of trouble nailing anything down.

For example, a lot of military records were destroyed during the blitz in the Second World War so those that remain are incomplete. Also there are a huge amount of Percy Evans that served in WW1 but none of them can be clearly identified as being our boy.

That is not completely unusual in itself as Percy's brother William was a major during WW1 but we can't find anything recorded about him either.

We know for a fact that he was a retired major as it is mentioned on the 1939 Census and also in later announcements relating to his WW2 service in the London Gazette. But we haven't been able to find out for definite when he enlisted, where he might have served or in which regiment he was a Major during the First World War.

Now, if we take Percy's timeline as being exactly as it was set out in the Denstone Register, then he may well not have served in the armed forces at all and may, indeed, have spent the war years working as a school teacher.

The only documentary proof of any of this comes from a reference to a letter that he wrote to "The Denstonian" school magazine in June 1916 where he states that he has failed seven times to get past the Medical Officer to join the Army.

Percy may well have had ill health or poor eyesight and had, instead, to make his contribution to the war effort by educating the next generation of citizens and brightening the place up with his art and poetry.

Percy Haselden's Writing

Percy Haselden published two collections of poems – both in 1917. He always used Percy Haselden as his pen name and not Percy Evans, which caused quite a lot of confusion while researching his background.

The first collection was called "Rhymes of Golden Days" (1917: Arthur H Stockwell, London), which we have not been able to locate and, therefore, know very little about.

The second was called "In The Wake Of The Sword" (Erskine Macdonald, London), which we HAVE been able to locate and are pleased to reproduce in full in the following pages.

His poem "Searchlights on the Mersey" was also published in "The Fiery Cross: an Anthology" edited by Mabel C. Edwards and Mary Booth and published by Grant Richards in 1915.

Haselden was clearly a keen and prolific poetry writer and he had verses published in numerous magazines and periodicals throughout the 1920s and 1930s. They are not very easy to track down but the ones that we have found have been included in chronological order in the latter section of the book.

Percy's Songs

1916: Devon Men

In 1916 Percy's poem "Devon Men" was set to music by Sir Charles Villiers Stanford (1852-1924), who was a very famous composer and conductor back in those days.

He was Professor of Music at Cambridge University and taught such promising students as Gustav Host and Ralph Vaughan Williams.

We are not quite sure how this musical collaboration came about. It could be that Stanford saw Haselden's poem published in one of the magazines that he used to send them to, and thought that it would work well as a song.

Or maybe Percy entered some sort of competition looking for rousing songs to support the war effort...

Whatever the set of circumstances, the music and lyrics and were published as sheet music by Enoch & Sons of London and the song appears to have been very well received.

1923: Spring Morning

In 1923, another of Percy's poems – " Spring Morning" - was set to music by Leigh Henry.

Leigh Vaughan Henry (1889-1958) was a Liverpool born composer, writer and conductor. He was working in Germany at the start of the First World War and ended up being interned as an enemy alien.

While in the prison camp at Ruhleben, Henry wrote an opera called "Moon Robbers." He escaped and reached the frontier disguised as a Prussian officer, carrying the score of his opera with him in a bundle of laundry. The opera was later performed in Germany and America.

With them being of similar age, coming from the same area and both being of Welsh backgrounds, there is more likelihood that Percy and Leigh might have known each other personally and, both being part of the arts and literature scene in the inter war years, they will have probably patronised the same festivals and events .

The finished song was published by Curwen and Sons of London and was used as test piece for the 1925 National Eisteddfod programme in the mezzo soprano solo competition.

"Spring Morning" was performed live on the 5WA Cardiff radio station (later BBC) on Tuesday 28th January 1928 at 7.45pm as part of a programme of "Welsh Composers – Original Works by Leigh Henry".

Henry himself conducted the Cardiff Station Orchestra while soprano Megan Talini sang the words to Percy's song.

1926: Mendip

Haselden's poem "Mendip" - which had previously appeared in Punch was set to music by somebody called Fred A Goudge in 1926 and published by Folk Press Ltd, London.

We don't really know very much about Fred Goudge as a songwriter – or how he came to be involved with Percy Haselden.

From what we can gather, Fred Goudge (born 1893) was the son of a colliery worker from Aspatria in Cumberland and his father, Henry Thomas Goudge, was quite well known in amateur circles as a band leader and conductor in the local area.

At the time of the 1911 Census, Fred is shown as living in Workington as a hairdresser with his brother in law - the shop owner, Robert Lightfoot - who Fred's older sister Jane had married in 1902.

The next thing that we know about Fred Goudge is from the Kelly's Local Directory for North and East Yorkshire for 1925, which states that he was a hairdresser with his own shop living in Bridlington

There are numerous mentions of a Fred Goudge in the Hull Daily Mail during the late 1920s and 1930s reviewing shows by the Bridlington Amateur Players, of which he appears to have been a prominent performer.

But that's all we can find out about him – assuming that this is the same Fred Goudge who wrote the music to Percy's verses, which does, at least, seem likely.

Folk Press Ltd of London seem to have been quite active in the 1920s and 30s and dealt with what we would probably describe these days as "niche" or vanity publishing.

They specialised in books about local history, folk traditions, superstitions, mythology and dialects, with a particular interest in Somerset, for some reason.

They produced a bi-monthly magazine in the mid 1920s called Word Lore which was described itself as "the folk magazine, a recorder of dialect, folksong, ballad, epigram, place name phrase and folklore".

Within the pages of Word Lore they regularly advertised for people to send in folk songs and "song poems" – whether published or unpublished – so this may have been how Percy's poem came to be published by them as a song.

Haselden's Last Published Work

The last work of his - that we can find any record of - is a song called "Unto His Majesty - We Hail You!", which was published by Independent Music Club, London in 1936.

Percy provided the words and the music was written by Margaret Meredith, who was a prolific composer of songs and religious music during the early half of the 20th century and a widely recognised expert on chamber music as well.

Here again, we haven't been able to locate a copy of the song to study it but, taking into account the timing of its publication, it would almost certainly have been in praise of the new King Edward VIII who assumed the throne in January 1936 upon the death of his father George V.

As Edward VIII only reigned for 11 months, causing months of constitutional crisis before finally abdicating in December 1936, it s not really hard to see why this song might have fallen out of fashion very quickly and is now long forgotten.

That's not to suggest that Percy never wrote anything else ever again – just that we haven't been able to find any mention of him anywhere. He lived on for another 23 years and, having spent most of his life writing poems and songs, it is really very unlikely that he would suddenly stop doing it from one day to the next.

At the time of the 1939, census he was still working as a teacher in Essex so it is not as if he had retired from public life – or been taken ill and residing in a nursing home.

In fact, the poems that we have reproduced in this book will only be a very small tip of very large iceberg. These are just the poems of his that have been published that we have been able to FIND.

There is a list in the back pages that includes published poems that we cannot (yet...) trace and there are likely to be many dozens - if not hundreds - more that were published somewhere or other in forgotten journals and magazines that have never been archived over the years and are impossible to find out about.

And what about all the poems that he wrote and sent off which never got published? There must be hundreds more of those. And anything that was a "work in progress" but never got finished?

If you have ever done any writing yourself – be it poetry or prose, fiction or fact – or if you have had any dealings with a serious writer, you will know that they are always jotting ideas down in notebooks, on scraps of paper, backs of fag packets, beer mats, restaurant napkins or whatever.

And that their house is overrun with these bits of paper with the odd line here, a few facts there, things to remember, things to check up on and lines and ideas to come back to and work on later.

With Percy having clearly written and published poetry over many decades, his house will have been full of these notes, ideas and word in progress. All of which will probably have been lost over time and we will never get to know about.

It is also sad that, despite him having been an art teacher and respected artist for all his professional life, there is no record or surviving example that we have been able to find of any of the hundred of artworks that Percy must have produced over the years.

If YOU know different – please get in touch!

Paul Breeze
Wallasey 2023

In The Wake Of The Sword

Originally published In 1917
by Erskine MacDonald Ltd, London

Dedicated To Rowland Thurnam MD

With affection

Belgium, 1914-1915

AGONY

NOW for a season lifted up,
The second cross—the gleaming
sword—
Proffers Thy lips a blood-filled cup—
This is Thy second Passion, Lord.

For Man, of old, Thy blood was shed ;
Man pours, to-day, his blood for Thee,
He hath not where to lay his head—
Behold this new Gethsemane !

DOUBT

God-like He suffered once for Man,
Man-like in bitter paths He trod ;
Shall we but find in Heaven's plan
Man suffers many times for God ?

HOPE

Ah ! no ; as from the clouded East
Rose the pale Star at eve to guide
The seers to their spotless Priest—
The Son of Woman deified—

So from the crimson clouds of War,
When these ill days begin to wane,
Hope shall arise, a glorious star,
To lead us unto Him again. . . .
Then shall prevail the Cross of Wood
Against this creed of Iron and Blood !

Cavalry in the French Vineyards

(Autumn, 1914)

OVER the land we thunder
   Crushing the fruitful vine,
Shaking the earth with wonder,
   Mingling blood and wine ;

Crushing the fruitful vine—
   Never shall glasses clink it ;
Mingling blood and wine—
   Only the earth shall drink it ;

Never shall glasses clink it,
   Friend pour out for friend,
Only the earth shall drink it—
   Such is the shapen end. . . .

Friend pour out for friend
   Naught but his blood beside him,
Such is the shapen end—
   Wine for the stones that hide him ;

Naught but his blood beside him
   Poured in the onward flight—
Wine for the stones that hide him,
   Wine for the worms' delight.

Poured in the onward flight
   Rivers of blood we scatter,
Wine for the worms' delight—
   Hearken the wine-press' clatter !

Rivers of blood we scatter :
  Mad ! we are mad to-day !
Hearken the wine-press' clatter
  Crushing the wine away !

Mad ! we are mad to-day !
  Over the land we thunder
Crushing the wine away,
  Shaking the earth with wonder !

Searchlights on the Mersey

A LONG lean bar of silver spans
    The ebon-rippled waterway,
And like a lost moon's errant ray
Strikes on the passing caravans—

Ghost-ships that from the desert seas
    Loom silent through the steady beams,
    Pale phantoms of elusive dreams
Cargoed with ancient memories.

Through the long night across the cool
    Black waters to their shrouded birth,
    Bearing the treasures of the earth,
Glide the fair ships to Liverpool.

Eastward Ho!

(A Song of Battle for when the German Fleet puts out of Kiel)

COMES the message, " Sailing westward
through the waterway of Kiel."
And we know their game is England, and
that's all we care to know :
So we watch our gallant flag-ship with its
ready hands of steel
Hoist the long-awaited signal, " Eastward
ho ! "

Eastward ho ! we thunder outward to the
gateway of the sun,
Outward, onward, ever striving through
the billows to the foe,
And we plough the jolly ocean, since there's
duty to be done,
Singing lustily and gladly, " Eastward
ho ! "

We will pluck the flying feathers from the
swooping eagle's wing
While the nations rally round us, while
the strident breezes blow
Far and wide our valiant slogan till the very
heavens ring :
God of Battle, shield and speed us
Eastward ho !

The New Pilate

(Two noteworthy incidents at the outbreak of
the war were the death of the Pope and the total
eclipse of the sun.)

YOU wash your hands in blood, you who
would show
The world your innocence: is it not told
How one with water cleansed his hands
of old
Crying, " Behold me innocent " ? And now
You call on God the while you crucify
Him in His children in the field of blood,
Your sword—grim token of the sacred
Rood—
Red with the blood of a new Calvary.

Even as of old earth trembles once again,
And though saints rise not now lo one
has died

Powerless to bring a savage world to grace ;
And as the darkness came when God was
slain
So now before the newly-crucified
The outraged sun has veiled his pallid
face.

Devon Men

FROM Bideford to Appledore the
meadows lie aglow
With kingcup and buttercup that flout the
summer snow ;
And crooked-back and silver-head shall mow
the grass to-day
And lasses turn and toss it till it ripen into
hay ;
For gone are all the careless youth did reap
the land of yore,
The lithe men and long men,
The brown men and strong men,
The men that hie from Bideford and ruddy
Appledore.

From Bideford and Appledore they swept
the sea of old
With crossbow and falconet to tap the
Spaniard's gold;
They sped away with dauntless DRAKE to
traffic on the Main,
To trick the drowsy galleon and loot the
treasure train ;
For fearless were the gallant hands that
pulled the sweeping oar,
The strong men, the free men,
The bold men, the seamen,
The men that sailed from Bideford and
ruddy Appledore.

From Bideford and Appledore in craft of
    subtle grey
Are strong hearts and steady hearts to keep
    the sea to-day ;
So well may fare the garden where the
    cider-apples bloom
And Summer weaves her colour-threads
    upon a golden loom,
For ready are the tawny hands that guard
    the Devon shore,
      The cool men, the bluff men,
      The keen men, the tough men,
The men that hie from Bideford and ruddy
    Appledore.

The Tyrolese Reaper

I

IT was most my life to dream and sing
     Away on the upland plain
Where I heard the silver cow-bells ring
As I gathered the ripened grain.

And girls came up from the little town
     (With a song and their lips for me)
To glean when the golden corn was down
And love while the world was free.

II

They fettered him with a loathsome pack
     And fastened a gun in his hands,
That he who had reaped should bend his
     back
To sow men's blood on the lands.

They mowed him down in the sleep of youth
     When his dreams were but begun,
And his body lies for the jackal's tooth
And rots in the harvest sun.

Cymru am Byth

(Saint David fought strenuously and successfully
against the heresies of his times)

LAND of the thousand valleys,
  Land of a thousand songs,
Each son of thine who dallies
To-day the trumpet rallies
  To join the dauntless throngs :
Of old thy sturdy Saint prevailed
Against unnumbered wrongs.

Land of a thousand battles,
  Land of a thousand bards,
Is there who minds his chattels
While Honour's war-drum rattles
  Across thine ancient shards ?
Of old thy sturdy Saint prevailed,
To-day his spirit guards.

Land of a thousand by-ways,
  Land of a thousand streams,
Southward along thy highways
Let Honour's ways be my ways—
  True path of song and dreams :
Of old thy sturdy Saint prevailed,
To-day his banner gleams !

Adventurers All

AUGUST fifteen-seventy-three,
Thunder of guns in Plymouth Sound,
DRAKE is home from the Golden Sea,
Back from the Isles of Wonder;
And this is the song that the loud guns sing,
Fresh from their wide adventuring,
" Who'll sail with us the whole world round
And chase the Don for plunder ? "

Sea-king ne'er lacked followers long,
Devonshire lads are first to go,
Stout hearts throb as the booming song
Heralds the grim sea-rover :
" O who will away with my hardy crew
In quest of lands where dreams come true ?
My culverin and gay crossbow
Have sung the wide world over ! "

DRAKE has found a mariner's bed
(Devonshire lads are like to rove),
Safe the sea keeps England's dead
Who roamed the oceans seven ;
And ever the wind over drift and tang
Sings as of old the cannon sang
When DRAKE came beating up the cove,
" Who sails *to-day* from Devon ? "

Nocturne

FRAIL shadows on the long straight road
   Fall from the pines that murmur spells
And stand like wizard sentinels
Before a fabulous abode ;

Above the hedge the crescent-moon
   Hangs like a slender scimitar,
   While cloud-looms weave a gaunt hussar
In battle with a strange dragoon ;

And from the topmost barren stem,
   As the fierce figures clash and fade,
   Behind a whirling cavalcade,
A throstle chants his requiem !

Song of Factors

("The trenches are not all in Flanders. Every city is
a labyrinth of trenches. Every workshop is a rampart:
every yard which can turn out munitions of war is a
fortress.

"Picks, shovels, lathes, hammers—they are as much
the weapons of this great war of European liberty as a
bayonet, a rifle, and a machine-gun."—Lloyd George.)

I SING the song of the delving spade
  That stalwart navvies wield,
The lathe that turns the hand-grenade,
  The plough that turns the field,
The hammers that fashion the swerving
    blade
  Or mattocks for a shield.

I sing the song of the artisan,
  The labourer with his hoe,
The forge that cleaves a path for man,
  The fields where harvests grow—
Swift hammers to fashion a giant plan,
  To smash a giant foe.

I sing the deft hands that labour well—
  Keen hands of skill and grit,
Moulders that shape the cunning shell,
  Men in the sullen pit—
All hammers to shatter the powers of Hell
  And break the gates of it !

To a Prisoner in Germany

(June, 1915)

WILD roses and campion,
The throstle's clarion,
Colour and sound and scent
In sweet conspiracy
Bringing our world content—
So, love, for you and me
Came summer a year ago. . . .
The flowers bring hope to-day,
And from each emerald spray
The dear shrill birds we know
Promise, when night is gone,
Wild roses and campion,
Damp summer scents in the lane
And you, dear, home again !

Flight

(Summer)

ABOVE the meadows, flower-strewn,
 A monoplane against the sky
Gleams like an amber dragon-fly
That skims an infinite lagoon ;

Over the slender aspen-trees
 On swift unerring wing it comes—
 The keen propeller whirs and hums
Like giant swarms of angry bees ;

High overhead it pulses on
 Westward into the waning light,
 And now within the web of Night
It dips, and wavers, and is gone !

To the Memory of a Brave Woman

I

I KNEW you not, pale sister, whose dear
    eyes
Had watched in tenderness beside the bed
Of those who suffered—heedless if they
    bled
For England or for England's enemies ;
Not yours to question whence those eager
    cries
    For comfort in their pain, each weary
        head
    Knew the kind arms that now lie still
        and dead
Beneath the star-decked cere-cloth of the
    skies.

I knew you not, but now the wide earth
    knows
    How the sick wolves have slain their
        comforter,
Biting the hand that fed them : not for
    long
    Shall these blind monsters vex the world's
        repose ;
    And through the ages shall you grow
        more fair,
" A name in story and a light in song ! "

Let there be light ! Dark shadows clog the
    sun
  While monstrous fingers clutch the help-
    less throat,
  And savage eyes burn red with lust and
    gloat
In elemental pride ; what powers have spun
The night beneath whose cloak this thing is
    done

  That shocks the world as if some devil
    smote
  The Mother of the Lord ? Do *they* not
    quote
The Scriptures to their purpose thus begun ?

Let there be light—each man a flaming
    brand
  To rout the beasts that war upon the
    weak
And martyr the mild hands that soothe
    their pain ;
  A clarion resounds throughout the land :
  Now let your swords, O men, in venge-
    ance speak,
That your strong hands shall bring us light
    again !

De Senectute

I WISH I were a boy again
  (The same as many a man must wish)
To ramble careless in the rain
  And scour the little stream for fish ;

To get up early with the sun
  And hear the birds that sing and shout,
To watch the rabbits start and run
  At seeing me so soon about ;

To wander, wander all the day,
  To filch the apples from the farm,
To get in everybody's way
  And dodge the dairy-wench's arm.

And most to-day I feel the lack
  Of youthful vigour in each vein
While England strides the thunder-track—
  I wish I were a boy again !

In a Book of Romances

(January, 1916)

LIKE some tired reveller I stray
  From surfeit of the world's mad dance
To hoarded dreams of yesterday
  In old-world gardens of Romance.

Here is a little dreamland hewn
  Out of the nigh-forgotten days
When knightly deeds and flowers of June
  Were meet for courtly ladies' praise ;

Here is a garden where still bloom
  Old-fashioned favourites that spin
Glad pictures for my silent room
  That Sorrow may not enter in.

To the Destroyer

(In many villages in Flanders the Crucifixes and statues of the Virgin and Child have escaped injury although the walls which sheltered them have been shattered.)

WHAT have you left undone? With
sword and flame
You slew the women for your Lord's
renown
And maimed the little ones that cried for
food ;
Yet in the temples builded in His name
Madonna still unwounded gazes down,
And Christ still hangs outstretched upon
the Rood!

Nunc et in Hora Mortis

O MOTHER of our Grace, Immaculate,
All-piteous human ward of human-
kind,
Thou whom the steadfast Magi thought
to find
In palaces, where ruled the sickly great
'Mid pallid pomp and circumstance of
State—
They found thee with thy Babe where
herd and hind
Were harboured, and thy patient hands did
bind
Scant linen round His body delicate. . . .

Shield us, pale Mother of the tear-stained
face,
Now and the when we lie unwrapt and
dead—

As thou didst swathe thy Son and kiss the
head,
Bleeding and bruised, that childishly had
lain
And slept within thine arms—lest we
remain
Unminded children of the market-place.

Merseyside

"Hamburg, and Bremen, and Antwerp are caught tight in the vice of war. Liverpool is as free and open as the great ocean from which it draws sustenance and strength." ("Times" Special Article.)

OH, Hamburg frets a desert-place, while Bremen quays lie bare,
For manacled their ocean-hounds rust in a sullen lair,
But free and strong fares Liverpool, proud daughter of the sea,
And strong the brown adventurers that keep the City free!

Three-score and seven winding miles the river tumbles down
To find the surging highway past the gates of Merseytown,
Three-score and seven laughing miles from where the pippit sings
Along the Moss at Featherbed, beside the meadow-springs.

It threads the hundred bridges as it snares the dozen streams
Before it laps the haven where the merchant stores his dreams,
Where glide the shallow barges and lean tramps that hug the bay,
And galleons that ply for gold a thousand miles away.

From ports that deal in thunder and from
isles that hoard the sun
To Liverpool the gay ships ride when each
long cruise is done,
And rich with spoil from every land the men
of Merseyside
Speed where the Rock Light points a road
across the snarling tide.

Three-score and seven silver miles the river
hurries down
To see the men of Merseyside sail in to
Merseytown ;

They hear the singing river boom its greet-
ing from afar,
That lisped in song at Featherbed and
thunders at the bar !

Note: The Mersey river rises in Featherbed Moss on the
borders of Derbyshire

Mendip

(A soliloquy in view of approaching leave)

ON Mendip, on Mendip, the gorse is
    amber now,
And dandelion torches attend the march
    of May ;
We Mendip men that coaxed the team and
    drove the sullen plough,
        No more we shout on Mendip,
        Dear golden, glowing Mendip,
    Oh, many leagues from Mendip is the
    land we cleave to-day.

On Mendip, on Mendip, the willow-creeper
    sings,
And bright birds and blackbirds and half
    a hundred more ;
The cuckoo's busy boasting of the trouble
    that he brings

        To feathered folk on Mendip—
        And soon I speed to Mendip
To nest awhile in Mendip with its fairy-
wonder store.

To Mendip, to Mendip, where boom the
    happy bells
From Blagdon and Burrington and Glas-
    tonbury town,
I'm coming by the willow-pools that fringe
    the road to Wells ;
      Oh, soon to breezy Mendip,
      To many-coloured Mendip,
    I'm coming back to Mendip just to wander
    up and down !

London Town

WHO will tilt for London Town, and
   who will run away ?
Come and join your fellows ! We are
   hearty, we are strong !
While the lasses revel in the lilac hours of
   May,
Wheeling from the meadows to the mur-
   mur of a song—
     " London, London,
     Wonder-weaving London,
Who would take me thither in my Cinderella
   gown ?
     London, London,
     Piccadilly London,
I will buy a lilac dress before I dance to
   Town ! "

Come and fight for London Town and wear
   a favour now
(Lilac for the ladies who would die for
   London too) ;
" Come," the blackbird carols from the
   nodding willow-bough,
   " Come, while I am trilling what a lady
   loves to you—
     London, London,
     Dilly-dally London,
Subalterns for lackeys and a major for my
   beau ;
     London, London,
     Busybody London,
Jealous eyes are prying as I canter in the
   Row."

Come and tilt for London, lad, until the foe
    is down,
  Come and join your fellows! We are
    hearty, we are strong !
Then to kiss the wayward girls who wait in
    London Town,

Lips awake with laughter and the ripple
    of a song—
      " London, London,
      Lads' and lasses' London,
Kisses without number for the boys who
    guard her well ;
      London, London,
      Merrymaking London,
Kisses for the sturdy boys—and they may
    kiss and tell ! "

The Golden Valley

(Herefordshire)

ABBEYDORE, Abbeydore,
   Land of Apples and of gold,
Where the lavish field-gods pour
   Song and cider manifold ;
Gilded land of wheat and rye,
Land where laden branches cry,
   " Apples for the young and old
Ripe at Abbeydore ! "

Abbeydore, Abbeydore,
   Where the shallow river spins
Elfin spells for evermore,
   Where the mellow kilderkins
Hoard the winking apple-juice
For the laughing reapers' use ;
   All the joy of life begins
There at Abbeydore.

Abbeydore, Abbeydore,
   In whose lap of wonder teems
Largess from a wizard store,
   World of idle, crooning streams—
From a stricken land of pain
May I win to you again,
   Garden of the God of Dreams,
Golden Abbeydore.

Collected Poems

by Percy Haselden

Printed in various publications between 1914 and 1930

With additional informative notes

Notes on Magazines and Journals

Punch

Punch Magazine, or "The London Charivari", was a British weekly magazine of humour and satire established in 1841 by journalist and playwright Henry Mayhew (25 November 1812 – 25 July 1887) and artist and wood-engraver Ebenezer Landells (1808 – 1 October 1860 London). Punch was particularly influential in the 1840s and 1850s, when it helped to coin the term "cartoon" in its modern sense as a humorous illustration.

At its peak in the late 1940s, Punch's circulation reached around 180.000. It ran from 1841 to 1992, was revived in 1996, but closed again in 2002.

The Westminster Gazette

The Westminster Gazette was an influential Liberal newspaper based in London. It was known for publishing sketches and short stories, including early works by Raymond Chandler, D. H. Lawrence, Katherine Mansfield and Saki and travel writing by Rupert Brooke.

The daily broadsheet paper ran from 1893 to 1928 and had a circulation of around 20.000.

Country Life

Country Life is a British weekly glossy magazine, based in London. It was launched in 1897 and is still published today. Its circulation in 2015 was 39.000.

The Windsor Magazine

The Windsor Magazine was a monthly illustrated publication produced by Ward Lock & Co in London from January 1895 to September 1939 (537 issues).

The title page described it as "An Illustrated Monthly for Men and Women".

The British Journal of Nursing

The British Journal of Nursing is a monthly medical journal covering nursing. In addition to academic material on nursing and hospitals, the journal provides information on people and events as well as photographs and advertisements.

There have been two versions of the journal. The original ran from 1888 to 1956 - being called The Nursing Record until 1902. The journal was revived by new publishers in 1992 and is still produced to this day.

The Living Age

The Living Age was an American weekly magazine comprising selections from various British and American magazines and newspapers. It was founded by Eliakem Littel in Boston, USA, in 1844 and ran until 1941.

Educational Times

The (London) Educational Times (A Review of Ideas and Methods) - was the Journal of the College Of Preceptors - founded in Britain in 1846 to standardize the teaching profession.

The College was closely linked to the Educational Times, a journal of "Education, Science and Literature" launched in 1847.

The journal appeared as "Educational Outlook and Educational Times" from 1924 to 1929 and then "Educational Outlook" from 1930 to 1932.

The Journal of the College of the Preceptors continue today under the title of "Education Today"

Time and Tide

Time and Tide was a British weekly political and literary review magazine founded by Margaret, Lady Rhondda, in 1920. It started out as a supporter of left wing and feminist causes and the mouthpiece of the feminist Six Point Group. It later moved to the right along with the views of its owner. It always supported and published literary talent.

The magazine ran from 1920 until 1979, becoming monthly from 1970. It was briefly resurrected as a quarterly between 1984 and 1986, published by Sidgwick and Jackson.

Despite featuring contributions from numerous very well known writers of the day, Time & Tide was always a niche publication – heavily subsidised by Lady Rhondda - and, at its peak, had a circulation of around 14.000.

EN PASSANT

LOUD swells the roar of traffic in the street,
The motor-buses rumble on and wind
Their plaintive warnings as they come behind
Faint folk who dally dazed by summer heat;
The reckless taxis seem a deal too fleet
To country cousins nervously inclined
And raucous newsboys fret the curious mind
With spicy rumours of the foe's defeat.

But suddenly a hush falls everywhere:
Stopp'd is each taxi with its languid load,
And, as the city's silence deeper grows,
Only a barrel-organ churns the air
While Peggy (in the middle of the road)
Pauses to put some powder on her nose!

Published in Punch, 26th August 1914

MOON-PENNIES

*(Children in the Midlands give this name to
the dis-shaped fruit of the plant Honesty.)*

MY garden is a beggar's pitch
That Heaven throws its coins upon;
And in the Summer I am rich,
And in the Winter all is gone;
Yet as the long days hurry by
I keep my pitch content and free,
Where in a sweet profusion lie
Fair Marigolds and Honesty;
And oft I turn and count for fun
My largess from the night and noon –
The golden tokens of the sun,
The silver pennies of the moon!

Published in Punch, 7th August 1914

Moon-pennies are the seeds of the Honesty plant

TO A POMPADOUR CLOCK

BRIGHT loves and tangled flowers
Adorn your china face;
You beat out silver hours
Within your golden case.

Still rings Old Time's denial
Of respite in your tone,
But o'er your p ainted dial
Is built a little throne –

A throne so neat and narrow
Where, heedless of your chime,
Poising his gilded arrow
Sits Cupid killing Time!

Published in Punch, 23rd September 1914

THE EGOIST

(From the French of Antoine Vincent Arnault)

Friendless and childless as well,
Below there he lives quite a stranger,
Hurrying into his shell
At the smallest suspicion of danger;
He loves himself only—too well,
He fills up his wee house alone,
He creeps out when Winter is gone
To flourish his horns at his neighbours;
In tracks of unsavoury slime
He leaves signs of his pestilent labours;
He'll ravish the loveliest bloom
With his kisses and venomous spume...
At last in his prison-like cell
He grows older and sadder with time.
This is an egoist's tale.
And the history, too, of a snail!

Published in the Westminster Gazette, 21ˢᵗ April 1915

A SKYLARK IN BIRDLIP MEADOWS.

Dawn kissed you, sweet bird.
Day broke and you stirred,
You sprang from your nest
To mingle your song with the light of the sun
Your medley of mirth And melody done,
You fell as a dart
To bury yourself in the breast of the earth
Your song in my heart.

Published in The Windsor Magazine, June 1915

THE ADVENTURER

IN Childhood's land of make-believe
　　I wandered long ago,
Content and keen to plan and weave
　　A constant shadow-show.

We prowled about like angry bears
　　Within the fire-guard den,
And stole doll children unawares
　　And rescued them again.

We'd blaze each chair-leg forest-tree
　　To balk an Indian plot,
Or sail into an oil-cloth sea
　　Upon the sofa-yacht;

We made our captives walk the plank
　　Across the nursery tray,
And wrecked the bath-ship on the bank
　　Of bricks in Carpet Bay.

But now, where City fetters cramp
　　My wayward feet, I slave;
Electric is Aladdin's lamp
　　The office is the cave.

Yet here, as in dear nursery days,
　　I roam adventuring,
And travel through unchartered ways
　　On Fancy's restless wing.

The marvels of the mystic East
I view in countless bales
While cunning merchants hourly feast
My ears on fairy tales.

The ledgers tell a wild romance
Of galleons strangely lost,
Of traders that have met mischances
When coral reefs were crossed.

The wisdom of a thousand climes,
The witchcraft of a few,
The glamour of the "good old times,"
The vigour of the new –

All these combine to weave for me,
Out of the rush and din,
Fair dreams of gallant days to be
And wonderlands to win.

Published in Punch, 11th August 1915

RHYMES OF GOLDEN DAYS

I.
The Lamplighter

When Peter gives the lamp a tap
With the tall wand he waves about,
He doesn't seem to mind a scrap
The lovely way a star comes out.

When he's made all the street-stars glow,
Nurse says that he goes home to bed;
If I could do such things I know
I'd stay and watch them shine instead.

II.
Tyranny

I hate to be told that I have to keep clean
'Cos somebody's coming to tea;
They only go talking to Mother and Jean
And never say nothing to me.

III.
Trees

The trees are shaking, so I know
It will be windy out today;
I see them scraping to and fro
And wearing the blue sky away.

Because I want to go to Town
They shake the wind and spill the rain –
If all trees could be cut down
There'd be no horrid storms again.

Published in Punch, 5th July 1916

Note from Lucy:

I remember I used to love watching the lamplighter light up the street lamps at dusk when we lived in Beckenham.

COLOURS

I HAVE ten colours in my box
And paint a lot of magazines,
And Mother's fashion-book of frocks
And picture-cards of kings and queens.

Of all my paints I'm fond of three
And hardly ever use the rest:
Yellow for fire, and blue for sea,
And red for soldiers – that's the best.

NOTE
I know they dress in khaki now,
But that's a colour hard to make –
The same as Mr Meadows' cow
That won't come right with crimson lake.

Published in Punch, 5th July 1916

MARCH.

Blithe March, the lusty troubadour, is here,
Singing by night and day loud serenades
To win the favour of the sweet young year.
For whom he has forsook all other maids;
And for a while she frowns upon his suit,
And pouts in buds that long refuse to blow,
For though he sing of hidden flower and fruit.
She still will toy with February's snow;
But when he's twenty-one the bright girl yields.
And throws a quick green mantle over her,
And trips to meet him through the woods and fields,
While fretful songs are found not anywhere.
And when they part before the April rains,
She flings her love a primrose for his pains.

Published in The Windsor Magazine, March 1917

THE CUCKOO

"In April come he will" the rhyme declares
That sings the cuckoo through hi English day
And children chant "In May he's come to stay
Through June he sings his tune" And travellers
Turn round the clinking contents of the purse
And wish for luck, fast ebbs his time away
For "In July he makes to fly" (they say)
"In August go he must " - so ends the verse

Oh, mocking and elusive troubadour
That wakes delightful panic in the breast
Hinting of sweets our English Aprils bold
Of gifts our English summer has in store
Why leave us were the harvest moon has blest
The laughing fruits, the hives of brimming gold.

Published in Country Life, 6th April 1918

THE TREES ARE SLAIN.

The sun's great lovers are the hills,
For him their breasts are bared amain;
No more the tyrant forest chills
Their shapely bosoms with his chain.
Now are they free to love again,
To fear "nor pine nor oaken bars,
To feel the soft lips of the rain
And traffic with the quiet stars.

Published in The Windsor Magazine, January 1919

AU BORD DE LA MER.
(Tenby, S. Wales).

The sea gleams like a jewelled tray
Where, in their matchless beauty, lie
The sapphire ribbons of the sky
Set cunningly to flout the day.
And now the wise, untramelled sun
Flings round a silver shaded veil
That masks the colours, thin and frail,..
Till sea and heaven seem as one.
And lazily the long day through,
The pale craft flit before my eyes,
Like silk embroidered butterflies,
Upon a satin screen of blue.

Published in the British Journal Of Nursing, 23rd August 1919

WISHING

Laughter in the orchard tells that fairy folk are there,
Dancing from the meadows of the moon;
Waving in the branches are the starlit wands they bear
Turn round seven times and beg a boon
Give me golden oranges,
Give me silver plums,
Give me moonlit honesty
To fashion fairy drums
If the first one doesn't hear you, ask the second one
that comes.
Over in the orchard, ere the day begins to break,
Sure you'll hear them singing if you're still.
Cross your little fingers when you see the nettles
shake;
Turn round seven times and say your will:
Change my sailing paper-boats
Into flying ships,
Throw me juicy wonderfruits
To press between my lips
Oh, you re bound to get your wishes if you don't make
any slips,

Published in The Windsor Magazine, July 1920

ROSEMARY ANN

Rosemary Ann, With your old-world name
You conjure up visions of delicate days:
Winsome patches, and flirt of fan,
And powdered popinjays put to shame
Who dared be lax in their ladies' praise.
Rosemary Ann, Do you have regrets
That you did not rule in those days of old,
To ride at ease in your rich sedan.
To punish, in one of your playful pets.
Some naughty nobleman overbold?
Rosemary Ann, Had you reigned a queen
And held battalions of hearts in thrall,
I would have craved, when your reign began.
To be your beau in that might-have-been.
To be the slave of your slightest call.
Rosemary Ann, How strange it seems
To watch you now as you careless loll
And pay no heed to the things 1 plan—
The golden days and the splendid dreams—
You're a wonderful name for a wooden doll.

Published in The Windsor Magazine, September 1920

THE OLD BEER FLAGON

(Many old English flagons are adorned inside with grotesque figures of animals.)

Within my foaming flagon
There craws with countless legs
A lazy grinning dragon
That wallows in the dregs,
Of old I saw him nightly
Look up with friendly leer,
As if to hint politely,
"I share your taste in beer!"

Through merry nights unnumbered
(From Boxing Day to Yule)
He'd greet me 'ere I slumbered
From out his amber pool;
But now he is beginning
To look a trifle strange,
His smile once wide and winning,
Has undergone a change.

No more, as pints diminish
(I wish the price grew less)
He hails me at the finish
With wonted cheeriness;
For, as I drain my mellow
Allowances of ale,
He seems to sigh, "Old fellow,
Will PUSSYFOOT prevail?"

Published in Punch, 3rd November 1920

A "FREE" KICK~ FROM A "FREE" COUNTRY.

This poem is about US prohibition laws, which were introduced in 1920. Apparently, there was an American prohibitionist campaigner called William "Pussyfoot" Johnson who visited Britain during 1919/1920 to support the temperance movement over here.

A lifelong foe of alcohol, he became active in the temperance movement in Nebraska in the 1880s. In 1906 President Teddy Roosevelt appointed him Special Agent in the Department of Interior to enforce laws in the Indian Territory and Oklahoma prohibiting sale of liquor to Native Americans.

He used a hand-picked group of deputies to aid him in stopping the liquor traffic. He served until 1911, smashing saloons and making over 4,000 arrests.

The Indians gave him the pet name Pussyfoot because he took to conducting his work at night in a very stealthy manner and was said to "pussyfoot" around at night.

(https://westervillelibrary.org/antisaloon-william-johnson/)

Johnson was a household name in the USA by the 1920s and he travelled for the World League Against Alcoholism, taking the dry message to numerous countries.

His 1919 visit to Britain provoked a huge public outcry and a concerted media campaign to support the British brewing industry and lots of posters and cartoons were produced to lampoon "Pussyfoot".

An alcohol free cocktail was created in 1920 by Robert Vermeire at the Embassy Club in London and named "Pussyfoot" after the campaigner.

According to Diffords Guide For Discerning Drinkers (www.diffordsguide.com), it consists of : 7 fresh mint leaves, 120ml orange juice, 15ml lemon juice, 15ml lime juice, 15ml grenadine syrup, & 1 egg yolk.

The modern day expression to pussyfoot comes from the soft steps of a cat. President Theodore Roosevelt popularized the term around 1905, using it to refer to men he believed were excessively cautious and sneaky.

However, the term was first used in the mainstream media in 1893 when it was used in the New York Scribner's Magazine to describe the Republican Convention of 1860 which nominated Abraham Lincoln as its presidential candidate. (www.wordorigins.org)

THE CLOUD

A cloud that capped the fir-clad hill
Changed fitfully to countless shapes,
Now clustered like a bunch of grapes,
Now like a face that threatened ill.

And once, when gilded by the sun,
A palace rose with sparkling domes,
Then vanished, and a troupe of Gnomes
Danced on roof tops one by one

And then an Alpine glacier,
Intent to carve the world below,
Loomed o'er the wood, and whirling snow
Shrouded and slew each pointed fir.

Published in The Living Age, 30th April 1921

APRIL SONG

Laps and lasses, list awhile
Unto this my song O!
Youth soon runs his pleasant mile,
Dreams don't tarry long O!
Lads and lasses, April lingers,
All too soon will Autumn claim us,
And shrill Winter's crooked fingers
Tear our garlands off and shame us.
Lads and lasses, heed my singing,
Haste to love lest sorrow
Set another tune a-ringing
Down the woods to-morrow.

Published in The Living Age , 28th May 1921

TO A BEE.

Bold vagrant of the yellow-buskinned feet,
Your busy day begins before the signs
Of wayside inns of thyme and meadowsweet;
And where the laggard host too long reclines
Within the lordly tavern of the rose,
With your loud tune you summon him to wake
And his fast petal-shutters to unclose,
And start the day's carousals for your sake.
Ah, it is wise, while Summer is your friend,
To take her timely gifts and store away
Food for rare feasts, that Winter shall descend
To find you proof against his evil day.
So grant that, when my days grow brief and cold,
I feed on hoarded dreams of summer gold.

Published in The Windsor Magazine, July 1921

TO SLEEP.
(From the French of Philip Desportes, 1546-1606.)

Come, Sleep, to my eyes again,
Beloved of gods and men,
Thou son of sweet Calm and Night
Who, soothing frail hearts that fret,
Dost croon to my cares, " Forget ! "
And conquer the hands that fight.
Come, Sleep, thou beloved one,
'Twas long ere the day was done,
And night is half-fled away,
And I lie a-waiting still
For thee to scatter the ill
Blind thoughts that have vexed my day.
Haste thou to come, oh Sleep !
Thee prisoner none may keep,
Nor even resist thy will , . . .
The watch-dog weary lies,
And the cock to no dawn cries,
And the wakeful goose is still.
But lo, I call thee alway
While the night ebbs fast to day
And the dawn's vermilion.
Ah, Love, my heart's tyrant king,
With a waft of thy errant wing
Thou hast beckoned to Sleep, " Begone ! "

.

Published in the Educational Times, August 1921

BEWILDERMENT.

I know not which is sweeter to the mind—
When the day's dying monarch leans upon
The world's grim edge before he quits mankind,
Or the first moment after he is gone.
Tell me, O bird that singest to my heart
From the kind leaves that temper the noon sun,
Does your proud singing make my tears to start,
Or the strange silence when your song is done ?

Published in The Windsor Magazine, November 1921

TRAMPING.

Out from the tyrant town we trod
To where the fields of freedom lay,
We saw dawn's lantern rouse the day,
And heard the lark remember God.
Dawn passed us bravely garlanded,
Not ragged as she comes to town.
The kingcups proffered her a crown,
A linnet praised her queenly head.
And now the bird of evening fills
This waiting world and heart of mine,
And night's soft raiment flows like wine,
In purple glory down the hills.

Published in The Windsor Magazine, June 1922

A CORNISH LANE IN SEPTEMBER.

Out of the foxglove's bell
Tumbles the drowsy bee,
Out of the monkshood cell
Into a meadowsweet sea.
Down the narrow lane
Rumbles the old hay waggon,
Brushing the hedges twain,
Crushing the wild snapdragon,
Bearing its fragrant load
Into the open road.
Ah, how good it seems
Just to be here again,
Harvesting April dreams,
Fearless of autumn rain
Dreams born anew to-day
Out of the scented hay.

Published in The Windsor Magazine, September 1922

THE CONQUESTS OF PEACE.
(FROM THE FRENCH OF ANDRE CHENIER.)

Flung from their lofty pedestals
Those spoilers of a thousand lands
That compass our proud city malls ;
They came with blood upon their hands
Fresh from the reeking sacrifice,
And stained with tears of blinded eyes.
Fall at the feet of nobler men
Who bear the cup of Liberty,
Who make the slave a citizen,
And reap where deserts used to be.
Purged of vain self themselves they give
That lon'lier men may laugh and live.
Grant them no cavalier applause
Who curb with health, whose ruling rods
Are freedom and ennobling laws;
Their names are numbered with the gods
Who would with loving hand and word
A nation from a nameless herd.

Published in The Education Outlook January 1924

THE MESSENGER.

Green drift transfigures all the hopeful trees,
For buds innumerable strive to break
In tender veils and kindly canopies-
Cool havens builded for each sweet bird's sake.
Begone, my cloak of Winter solitude
Lo, while triumphant voices wake and sing,
The woodpecker, impatient of my mood.
Taps for my heart to open to the Spring

Published in The Windsor Magazine, February 1924

THE JAZZ CANNIBAL

My Phillida, before the jazz
Began its devastating boom,
My thoughts of you were gentle as
The tunes that whirled us around the room
To perfect harmony with grace
We moved, delighted and content
To smile into each other's face
With meanings kind and innocent

Alack! My Phillida, today
The music does not soothe my mind
In truth I am compelled to say
My dreams are horrid and unkind;
For, while the bawling niggers biff
The drums that agitate our fee,
I'm gravely speculating if
You're really nice enough to eat.

Published in Punch. 10th December 1924

In his book "Jazz Poetry: From the 1920s To The Present", (Praeger: Westpost Connecticut. 1997) Sascha Feinstein writes:

> On January 10, 1925, Literary Digest reprinted "The Jazz Cannibal," a poem that had appeared overseas in Punch magazine the previous December and that was later credited to Percy Haselden.
>
> It begins with this epigraph from a letter printed in The Daily Graphic:
>
> *"The noisy beats of jazz-bands are merely a disguised and modern form of the tom-toms of old, which incited Savages to fury and fired the fierce energy of cannibals"*
>
> This disturbing narrative, which attempts to be clever and witty, offers little substance apart, perhaps, from the bizarre point of view.
>
> As a poem, "The Jazz Cannibal" should be dismissed, but historically it is of interest because it exemplifies the attitude at that time of many poets who were not unknown.

CROOKED CORNER

WHEN I pass Crookèd Corner
I hardly make a sound
Because I know the fairies
Have there a dancing ground;
And I've been shown the pixy throne
On which their queen is crowned.

And once by Crookèd Corner
I saw a russet cloak
Just slipping through the hedgerow
Beside the haunted oak;
Nurse told me then it was a wren,
I'm sure it was "The folk."

Someday by Crookèd Corner,
If I am very good,
Maybe I'll see the goblins
Come trooping from the wood;
I may myself become an elf –
I wonder if I could?

*Page 60, "Child Verses from "Punch" with drawings by Phyllis
Chase (J. Saville & Co., Ltd., London, 1925)*

A SONG IN SEASON.

Oh, April days,
Since you are here,
Love Cometh soon
With tears and laughter—childish ways;
March hummed a tune
We wearied of,
But now we heed
Pan with his wistful river-reed.
Piping of Love
Since you are here,
Oh, April days!

Published in The Windsor Magazine, April 1926

JUNE

Hear the sound of summer revelry
Steal from the orchards where the thriftless
May Lies 'neath his pall of blossom ;   far away
Unto the wakeful bosom of the sea
Wind the shrill notes of panic melody
To break the slumber of the yellow bay—
And where I marvel in the tumbled hay
Echoes from sea and valley come to me.
So through this day that bird-enchanters weave
My heart is cleansed with song, and semi-tone
Of whispering trees ;   and now, in wonderment,
I mark the coming of the hooded eve
When all the voices that the day has known
Sink to the perfect silence of content.

Published in The Windsor Magazine, June 1926

THE FOUR WINDS.

The North Wind scars the forest track ;
Blind in the fury of his haste
He lays the world-wide garden waste.
The South Wind lures the swallow back,
The dandelions' brazen shields,
And day-pied carpets for the fields.
The East Wind with his ivory fangs
Snaps at the lily as he strides
Snarling along the river -sides.
The West Wind in her frolic hangs
Bright garlands in the orchard -close
And to my garden flings a rose !

Published in The Windsor Magazine, July 1926

SLUMBER.

Threads of darkness clog the meadows,
Snare the daisy-dappled grass
Where the thin wind -drifted shadows
Wave, and break, and pass.
Silence now ; no late bird lingers ;
Drowsy nods each golden -cup
When the sky -man's filmy fingers
Shuts the poppies up.

Published in The Windsor Magazine, August 1926

TO A BEE.

O vagabond bee,
Trim, yellow-buskined mime,
By wayside inns
Of meadowsweet and thyme
Your busy day begins ;
With your loud tune
You tempt each laggard host
To open soon;
No matter who may keep
The tavern of the rose,
Wild rose, or bedded fair
Snug in the garden-close,
From their fond sleep
Your tune untimely rouses
And bids them stir
To start the day's carouses;
Insistent troubadour,
When the unshuttered leaf
Declares the fragrant store
Is open for the day
Your tarrying is brief,
There at your need
You drain its bowl of mead,
Then merry turn away
To other brews that wait
Beyond each petal-gate,
O vagabond bee !

Published in Country Life, 21st August 1926

THE WINTER WIND.

The wind is worrying the trees,
Wolf- craftily he paws them down,
The sunset is a crimson frown
Across the visage of the seas ;
Cruel wolf, like blood that's spilled
The last leaves trickle from your jaws.
Beneath your buried fangs and claws
Lies the slain forest, gaunt and chilled.
Yet from your caverns of the snow
Shall leap the cunning green of spring
To strangle you, and birds shall sing
The wonder of your overthrow !

Published in The Windsor Magazine, December 1926

ALADDIN'S GAMP

*(A French abbé is reported to be able to divine
the presence of gold and other precious metals by the
means of a rod composed of the ribs of an
umbrella.)*

WHENE'ER my lady rain
Trips boldly down the street,
I flaunt my gamp again
And plod on skidding feet
To plan how I may dodge the Fates
And win my daily bread and cates.

Had I the abbé's power,
How deft would be my way
To cull in one sweet hour
Sufficient for the day,
To conjure up long-hidden dibs
By waving my umbrella ribs!

Published in Punch, 15th December 1926

*(cate – noun – ARCHAIC plural noun: cates:
a choice dainty food; a delicacy.)*

THE MOON MAN

There's a man in the moon to attend to the light
And I'm sure he's asleep after cleaning it twice
Cos I saw it all shining on Saturday night
And now it is only a thin melon slice

Every time there's a moon, he plays just the same trick,
And appears to forget what he's thinking about.
Else he loses the scissors for trimming the wick –
But I wonder who wakes him and tells him it's out?

Published in Time and Tide and reproduced in a number of other periodicals such as The Brethren Evangelist (Ashland, Ohio), 7th January 1928

MODEL ADVICE

*(Mannequins are now being advised to give up slimming
exercises and food, so that their figures may become plumper
to fill the fuller costumes which are becoming fashionable.
Good meals with plenty of beer are advocated.)*

TIME was (and it was not remote)
When, Phyllis, you tabooed
The very thought of *table d'hôte*
Or *any* hint of food;
A lemon and a skipping rope
Were then your constant friends
Who made you like a telescope
To further Fashion's ends.

But, now that fashion turns and frowns
Upon the lean and lithe,
The fat alone in roomy gowns
Make jealous neighbours writhe;
So, Phyllis, to your steak and chips
And cheese and lollipops;
Forsake your little daily skips
And take a lot of hops!

Published in Punch, 31st December 1930

(Hops presumably referring to drinking 'plenty of beer'...)

REVIEWS AND OTHER PRESS CUTTINGS

The Bookman, August 1913
Honourable mention for an entry to a 21 Guinea Poetry
Competition to Percy Haselden, New Brighton (Poem not
printed)

Catalogue of Copyright entries 1916:
Devon Men words by Percy Halseden usic by Charles
Villiers Stanford Enoch & Sons London c 31st jan 1916

Dundee Courier, 4th December 1916 (re: Devon Men)
Sir Charles Stanford is the best musical painter of seascapes
that we have. The words are vigorous and picturesque and
the music has a real tang of the sea in it.

The Queen, 6th January 1917
An altogether delightful song, fresh too, is Devon Men by
Charles V Stanford to words of Percy Haselden (taken from
Punch). The breeziness of it all is quite in the composer's
true vein excellent in every way.

The Graphic, 28th July 1917
Rhymes of Golden Days. By Percy Haselden. (Arthur H.
Stock well.) 6d.

A series of 21 little poems dedicated in an admirable sonnet
to the author's mother. The poems that follow are in the
manner of Stevenson's "Child's Garden". The verses on the
colour box end plaintively in the fact that "they dress in
khaki now, but that's a colour hard to make – the same as
Mr Meadow's cow that won't come right with crimson lake"

The Scotsman 11ᵗʰ Oct 1917

Two neatly printed pamphlets of poetry (each 1s net) have been sent out by Mr Erskine Macdonald , London . One belongs to the series "The Little Books of Georgian Verse" and contains two-and twenty short lyrical poems by Mr Percy Haselden, collectively entitled "In the Wake of the Sword" .

They sing strongly and impressively about sorrows and hopes occasioned by the war and display a peculiarly heartsome spirit when praising fighting men from Devon , and when sketching the look of Liverpool and the Mersey in war-time.

The Atheneum, December 1917

Haselden, Percy: In The Wake Of The Sword (The Little Books of Georgian Verse) Erskine Macdonald, 1917. 7in 48pp, 1/n

An element of freshness is apparent in the author's treatment of some aspects of what is becoming a well-worn theme – the War. "Cavalry in the French Vineyards (Autumn 1914)", "Searchlights on the Mersey" and "The New Pilate" are good examples of Mr Haselden's style. "Merseyside" is also pleasing.

The Literary Yearbook 1921 (George Routledge & Sons)

HASELDEN , Percy; Black - and - White Artist, and Journalist . Au . of In the Wake of the Sword (Erskine Macdonald) , 1917 ; Rhymes of Golden Days (Stockwell) , 1917 ; C. To Punch, Sunday Times, Westminster Gazette, Windsor Mag, Colour etc   Willowgarth, Rose Valley, Brentwood Essex. (See also under Illustrators).

Catalogue of Copyright entries 1923:
Spring Morning - words by Percy Haselden music by Leigh Henry   Curwen & Sons London C 7th may 1923

The Musical Times of 1st December 1923:
Review of new songs published

Oddly, one of the most conventional songs of this batch and one showing in its harmony strong traces of the hated Teutonic convention is by Leigh Henry! It's only a very little one—a setting of a two-verse poem by Percy Haselden called Spring Morning (Curwen). An even worse convention—Mr. Henry ekes out his musical phrases by repeating words with bad effect, eg, ' Songs in the river's lisping purl, the River's purls.

And "In the heart a sweet content, in the heart content. No mean lyric poet himself, Mr Henry should know better than this!

Western Mail, 31st January 1925
Another work by Mr Leigh Henry also figures in the coming National Eisteddfod programme – a song Spring Morning to verses by another Liverpool Welshman Percy Haselden (PH Evans) which hahs been selected as a test piece for the mezzo soprano solo competition.

Somerset Standard, 17th Dec 1926

Mendip words by PH and music by Fred A Goudge. A notable addition to the songs in praise of Somerset. Published by Folk Press Ltd, London. Poem previously in Punch

The Denstone Register 1870-1930, ed: ET Greenwood MA (Wilding & Son Ltd, Shrewsbury 1932)

Swineshead, Lincoln, '23.

*HASELDEN, PERCY HASELDEN [late EVANS, P. H.], 32 *Warley Mount, Brentwood, Essex*. iv.—Div. (July '03) ; H.M.H. Liverpool School of Art '04–'12 ; National Award '11 ; Art Master Wallasey Gram. School '09–'20 ; Brentwood School since '20 ; published *In the Wake of the Sword* (Macdonald) '17 ; Contributor to *Punch, Country Life, Sunday Times, Outlook*, etc., and included in the following Anthologies : " Poems from *Punch* " (Macmillan) '21, " Child Poems from *Punch* " (Saville) '26 ; " The Fiery Cross " (Grant Richards) '16 ; Exhibited at Liverpool and Southport Exhibitions.

HOLLINGWORTH GEORGE HARRY. i.—('02) ; H.M.H.

Who's Who In Literature 1934 (Literary Year Books Press, Liverpool)

HASELDEN , Percy . B. 1886. Black - and - White Artist, and Journalist . Au . of In the Wake of the Sword (Erskine Macdonald) , 1917 ; Rhymes of Golden Days (Stockwell) , 1917 ; Child Poems from Punch (Seville) , 1926 ; C. Punch, Sun, Times, Windsor Mag etc 32 Warley Mount Brentwood Essex ...

(similar entry for several other years - Address given as Ongar Road in 1926 and 1928 editions)

Dictionary of British Art 1976 (Antique Collectors Club)

Haselden, Percy   Exh 1926
32 Warley Mount, Bentwood, Essex   † L1

Haselden, Percy (fl. 1910s-1920s) (chron.)
* Au Bord de la Mer (Summer), (pm) Colour February 1916
* Au Bord de la Mer (Tenby, S. Wales), (pm) Colour August 1919
* Bewilderment, (pm) The Windsor Magazine November 1921
* A Cornish Lane in September, (pm) The Windsor Magazine September 1922
* Flight (Summer), (pm) Colour May 1916
* The Four Winds, (pm) The Windsor Magazine July 1926
* Impression du Soir, (pm) Colour May 1916
* June, (pm) The Windsor Magazine June 1926
* March, (pm) The Windsor Magazine March 1917
* The Messenger, (pm) The Windsor Magazine March 1924
* Mills, (pm) The Merry-Go-Round October 1924
* The Passing of Lydia, (hu) The Humorist #1, July 29 1922
* A Post-Impressionist Landscape, (pm) Colour May 1918
* Rosemary Ann, (pm) The Windsor Magazine September 1920
* The Signal, (pm) Colour February 1916
* A Skylark in Birdlip Meadows, (pm) The Windsor Magazine September 1915
* Slumber, (pm) The Windsor Magazine August 1926
* To a Bee, (pm) The Windsor Magazine July 1921
* To My Laughing Lady, (pm) Colour March 1917
* Tramping, (pm) The Windsor Magazine July 1922
* The Trees Are Slain, (pm) The Windsor Magazine January 1919
* The Winter Wind, (pm) The Windsor Magazine December 1926

____, trans.

* Zodomirsky's Duel by Alexandre Dumas, (ss)
The Argosy (UK) August 1936; translated from the French
("Marianna", Herminie and Marianna, Méline, Cans et Cie.,
1859).

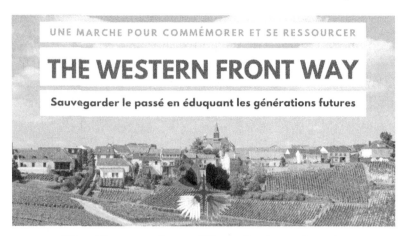

UNE MARCHE POUR COMMÉMORER ET SE RESSOURCER

THE WESTERN FRONT WAY

Sauvegarder le passé en éduquant les générations futures

The Western Front Way – by Lucy London

The Western Front Way is a new, continuous, permanent, marked path from the Swiss border in the South through France and Belgium to the channel coast in the North.

The path for peace is a memorial conceived by Rory Forsyth and inspired by a letter home from the Front during the First World War, sent in 1915 by Alexander Douglas Gillespie, who saw a time after the conflict and a way of healing the ravages of war. He wrote:

"... when peace comes, our government might combine with the French government to make one long avenue between the lines from the Vosges to the sea...a fine broad road in the 'No Mans Land' between the lines, with paths for pilgrims" .

Interestingly enough, Stanley Casson also contemplated the idea of such a pathway back in his 1935 book "Steady Drummer", when he wrote:

"Night in the trenches was the most enduring experience of all. I used to wonder how long it would take me to walk from the beaches of the North Sea to that curious end of all fighting against the Swiss boundary."

The Logo adopted by The Western Front Way depicts the four flowers of remembrance:

The Cornflower (bluet), which is the remembrance flower of France, the Daisy (madeliefje) of Belgium, the Forget-me-Not (Vergiss-mein nicht) of Germany & The Red Flanders Poppy

The use of the poppy is universal but the original idea of using it as a symbol of remembrance comes from American Poet Moina Belle Michael's vow always to wear a red poppy in remembrance.

The Western Front Way have just announced that you can purchase a marker with the 4 flowers of commemoration for France, Germany, Belgium & The Commonwealth for £5 and be a legacy for collaboration and peace.

Visit their website & find out how to order your waymarkers: https://www.thewesternfrontway.com/

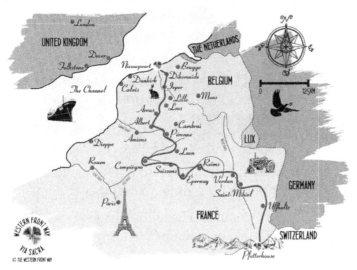

WALLASEY - DAYS GONE BY

TONY FRANKS-BUCKLEY

Wirral Historian and writer Tony Franks-Buckley organises The Thursday Evening Myths & Legends Tours in New Brighton, Wirral, UK for people to find out more about the Hidden History of Wallasey.

WALLASEY -
DAYS GONE BY
TONY FRANKS-BUCKLEY

Including:

New Brighton Ghosts of the Old Town Tour

Bidston Hill Ghosts, Witches and Folklore Tour

New Brighton Back In Time Tours

The History of The Gunpowder Village and Mother Redcaps Tour

New Brighton Smugglers Trail

For more information and bookings, visit:
https://poulton-creamery.sumupstore.com/

Check out the Facebook page at:
https://www.facebook.com/WallaseyHistoryBook/

Or buy the book via Amazon and elsewhere
ISBN: 978-1481109000

Rathbone Studio, 28 Argyle St, Birkenhead CH41 6AE

Part of the iconic Della Robbia Pottery was situated at 28 Argyle Street, Birkenhead, between 1894 – 1906. The ethos behind the Della Robbia Pottery was to bring individuality to each piece produced; allowing the artist to express and create unique and original designed ceramic work. Rathbone Studio aims to bring back the zeitgeist spirit of the Della Robbia Pottery to Birkenhead.

Studio and GalleryPottery workshops on the Wirral. Weekly pottery sessions, afternoon and evenings. See pottery workshop page for more details. Taster pottery session also available on Saturday morning, Sunday afternoon and Monday daytime for up to two people. Have a go at the potters wheel.

Enquiries to: potteryaware@hotmail.com

http://www.rathbonestudio.com/

"At The Going Down of the Sun" a collection of poems inspired by conflict and written by Becky Bishop

ISBN: 978-1727480788

Reviewed by Lucy London

I have loved reading books of poems since I was a little girl and, like Becky, I also write poems, some of which have been inspired by the loss of family members during wars.

Becky, however, brings a wealth of tradition to her work, because she is related to WW1 soldier poet brothers the Hon. Julian Grenfell (1888 - 1915), and The Hon. Gerald William Grenfell (1890 – 1915), and to their sister, the Hon. Monica Grenfell who served as a Red Cross nurse during the First World War. And, among the 485 relatives Becky's family lost due to conflicts, is also the WW1 soldier poet the Hon. Ivar Campbell (1890 - 1916).

Becky's poems are written from the heart and I found them at the same time moving and inspiring. Becky has exactly captured the mood of those of us who have relatives who were lost due to conflict but have no known grave upon which to leave flowers. Many of the poems are dedicated to a particular soldier, which I think is the most wonderful way of ensuring their memory lives on.

Beautifully illustrated throughout with Becky's own photographs from her visit to the Battlefields of the Western Front, this book should, to my mind, be required reading for every school pupil in order to remind them why we wear poppies in November each year. I would also hope that all the WW1 museums wherever they are would have copies, so that Becky's poems could be read at commemorative ceremonies.

Becky is a very prolific writer and I know she has a book of short stories due out soon – I can't wait to read them. To find out more about Becky's work please visit her website

https://beckyspoemsandbooks.wordpress.com/

Lucy London, July 2020

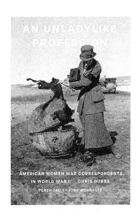

"An Unladylike Profession: American Women War Correspondents in World War 1" by Chris Dubbs (Potomac Books, Nebraska, 2020)

Reviewed by Lucy London

If, like me – in spite of having commemorated the First World War for years – you thought that the role of women during that conflict was to stay at home, knit and "keep the home fires burning", then this book is definitely for you!

Many of the exploits of the American women (and 1 British) journalists who braved the dangerous, U-boat infested waters of the Atlantic to travel to Europe during WW1 are, to say the least, hair-raising.

I found so much of interest in Chris's magnificent book that I could write a very long review – but that isn't the point as reviews need to be fairly brief.

The front cover – a photograph of photojournalist Helen Johns Kirtland inspecting an exploded naval mine on the Belgian coast - sets the scene, heralding Chris's research into the remarkable exploits of 39 women writers.

Due to my research during the centenary years for a series of commemorative exhibitions about the role of women in WW1, I already knew about Nelly Bly, Inez Milholland Boissevain and Louise Bryant but I had never heard of the others.

As well as quoting from the reports sent back to the various newspapers and magazines in America, Chris also tells us a good deal about the women themselves and includes photographs of the journalists, some of whom were not young women when they set out on their incredible journeys.

With superb illustrations, maps and biographies of the women journalists, plus a very detailed and impressive bibliography, this is a book you will return to again and again.

I could not put this book down, and I read it from cover to cover with great enjoyment. You must read it. With thanks to Chris Dubbs for a truly remarkable book and for mentioning me in the acknowledgements for Chris contacted me during the preparation of the book about some of the events included.

Lucy London, October 2020

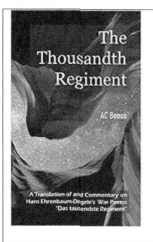

"The Thousandth Regiment: A Translation of and Commentary on Hans Ehrenbaum-Degele's War Poems" by AC Benus poet, writer and editor

by AC Benus (AC Benus, San Francisco, 2020)

ISBN: 978-1657220584

Reviewed by Lucy London

This book is a fascinating read and the poems are wonderful and have been beautifully translated. I am glad to say the original poems are also included.

Hadrian Bayley - The Man Who Accepted the Surrender of Jerusalem (Paperback)

ISBN: 9781838116514 £19.99

The war diaries of Hadrian Bayley covering both the Boer War and the First World War, telling the truth behind his accepting the surrender of the city of Jerusalem and having to give the keys back so a more senior officer could take the credit.

The City Of London Yeomanry 1907-1918

ISBN: 9781445664682 £27.99

For enquiries: +44 7702035951

stuartlatham65@sky.com

Stanley Casson
POEMS & PROSE

Compiled by Lucy London / Edited by Paul Breeze

With a foreword by Lady MacLellan

ISBN: 978-1-909643-50-5

Stanley Casson (1889-1944) was never actually a professional soldier – he was by profession an archaeologist and academic - and he only ever donned uniform in time of war to answer the call of his country in the two World Wars of the 20th Century.

This volume represents an overview of the life and writing of Stanley Casson.

Full Contents List:

Foreword by Lady MacLellan

How It All Came About by Lucy London

War Poems by Stanley Casson (2001)

A Brief Biography Of Stanley Casson by Lucy London

Stanley Casson And Rupert Brooke by Lucy London (2015)

Rupert Brooke And Skyros by Stanley Casson (1921)

A Few Words About Phyllis Gardner by Paul Breeze (2021)

Preface to "Progress of Archaeology" by Stanley Casson (1934)

Review of Steady Drummer by Lucy London (2021)

Review of Murder by Burial by Paul Breeze (2021)

A Lost Hero Of The Authors' Club by CJ Schuler (2018)

Death In Mysterious Circumstances by Paul Breeze (2021)

Mystery Flight:- Royal Air Force Squadron 525, Vickers Warwick C Mark I, BV247 by the Wartime Heritage Association

Stanley Casson on WorldCat

Bookshelf: More Reviews & Recommendations

WAR-TIME MEMORIES IN VERSE

WRITTEN WHILE OVERSEAS
BY SIGNALLER FRANK P DIXON

Originally privately published in 1937 in Canada
by his mother Ellen M Dixon

An annotated and illustrated 2022 reprint with new foreword by Lucy
London, biography, appendices and additional illustrations.

Edited by Paul Breeze

Full Contents List:

Foreword to the
2022 Edition by Lucy
London

Family Background
& Brief Biography

Commentary by
Steve Glover, Barrie
Legion Historian

Facsimile Reprint of
1937 Edition

Frank Dixon's Final
Resting Place

The Elkhorn
Monument

Jon Brooks –
"Cigarettes"

Appendices,
Information &
Recommendations

ISBN: 978-1-909643-52-9

War-Time Memories in Verse was originally published privately in Canada in 1937 by Ellen M Dixon

This edition reprinted in 2022 as a centenary reissue, revised and expanded edition with a new foreword, a number of new photographs and illustrations, new additional back pages by Posh Up North Publishing, New Brighton

Also from Lucy London....

Artists Of The First World War

Poets' Corners In Foreign Fields

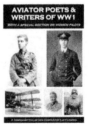

Aviator Poets & Writers

Female Poets V1

Female Poets V2

No Woman's Land

The Somme 1916

Arras, Messines, Passchendaele

Women Casualties – Belgium & France

Wilfred Owen: Centenary

Lucy London Songbook

The Adventures of Bunny, Archie, Alice & Friends

NADJA

THE COMPLETE POEMS

Edited by Paul Breeze / Foreword by Lucy London

THE NADJA MALACRIDA SOCIETY

ISBN: 978-1-909643-42-0

Full Contents List:

Foreword by Lucy London

Armistice day Letter to Nadja 2014

Nadja Malacrida – A Brief Biography

St Dunstan's

The Royal Star & Garter Home

The Evergreen: Poems (1912)

Love And War (1915)

For Empire And Other Poems (1916)

The Full Heart: Poems (1919)

Amy (1934)

Appendix: Bookshelf

Annotated and illustrated with a new introduction & preface, author biography, appendices and 12 new photographs. 2020 marks the 125th anniversary of the birth of the Marchesa Nadja Malacrida – or Louisa Green as she was born.

These four original collections were all written over a century ago and have been practically unobtainable for many years without laying out a small fortune to a rare book dealer.

We have put them together here with a brief biography of the author, and a few photos and other bits and pieces, that we hope you will find of interest – and that Nadja herself would also approve of.

Available by mail order from the Nadja Malacrida Society, poshupnorth.com, Amazon - and all other quality outlets.

MILITARY MUSEUM SCOTLAND

Set up by Ian Inglis, Military Museum
Scotland is Scotland's newest Museum.
It is a hands-on museum where visitors
get to handle most of the artefacts.
There are indoor and outdoor displays.
There is also a Cafe and Gift shop and
wheelchair access.

Opening Hours:
Tuesday – Sunday 10.00 – 16.00
Monday reserved for school visits only.

Military Museum Scotland,
Legion Hall, Louis Braille Avenue,
Wilkieston, Kirknewton,
West Lothian EH27 8DU

Contact Ian Inglis via e-mail: milmussco@yahoo.com

Facebook: https://www.facebook.com/milmussco/

https://www.visitscotland.com/info/see-do/military-museum-scotland

In the United States of America, Keith Arden Colley curates the WW1 Mobile Military Museum.

They have many settings and setups.

E-mail:
keithsmobilemuseum@yahoo.com

Website:
www.ww1mobilemuseum.com/

Twitter: @WWImobilemuseum

Facebook:

Awakening the Mind Mobile Museum
www.facebook.com/WWImobilemuseum

THE TEE ROOM

Where a Tea Room sits side by side with the wonderful world of golf!

172 Banks Road, West Kirby CH48 0RH
Tel: 0151 625 1887 / www.theteeroom.co.uk

The Tee Room is a 24 seater English Tea Room engulfed in a world of golfing bliss and you can find us on Banks Road in West Kirby.

We can seat 24 people and serve everything from breakfasts to traditional afternoon tea. We also have 10 different type of leaf tea, ranging from Traditional English Tea to Lovers Leap & Japanese Green Tea.

You'll always find a warm friendly atmosphere and we pride ourselves on the experience we like to offer our customers.

Ashville FC

Cross Lane, Wallasey
CH45 8RH

1st Team, Reserves, Ladies
& Junior Football

www.ashvillefc.com

@ashvillefc

Tel: 0151 903 3821

Poulton Creamery
Breakfast & Wrap Bar

393 Poulton Road,
Wallasey CH44 4DF

Tel: 0151 216 8814

https://poultoncreamery.
weebly.com

Home of The Hogfather Belly Buster - Breakfasts, Burgers, Hot Wraps
and Homemade Meals

Wilfred Owen's Wirral

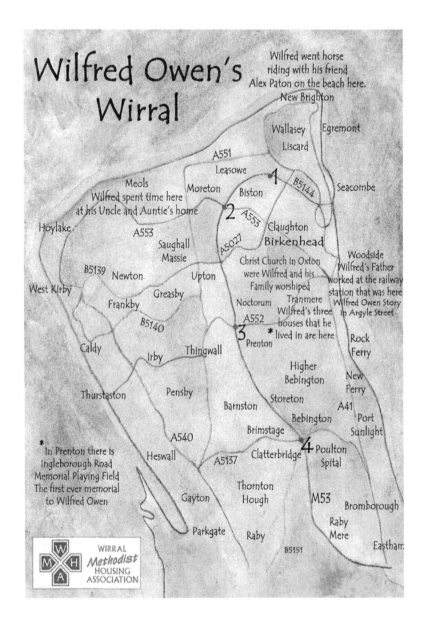

Wilfred went horse riding with his friend Alex Paton on the beach here.

New Brighton

Wallasey Egremont

Liscard

A551

Leasowe

Meols

Moreton Biston

Wilfred spent time here at his Uncle and Auntie's home

Hoylake

A553

Saughall Massie

Newton

West Kirby

B5139

Frankby

Greasby

B5140

Caldy

Irby Thingwall

Upton

Seacombe

B5144

A553

Claughton

A5027 Birkenhead

Christ Church in Oxton were Wilfred and his Family worshiped

Nocturum Tranmere

A552

Prenton

Woodside
Wilfred's Father worked at the railway station that was here
Wilfred Owen Story in Argyle Street

Wilfred's three houses that he * lived in are here

Rock Ferry

Higher Bebington

New Ferry

Thurstaston

Pensby

Barnston

Storeton

Bebington

A41 Port Sunlight

Brimstage

A540

Heswall

A5137 Clatterbridge

Poulton Spital

* In Prenton there is Ingleborough Road Memorial Playing Field The first ever memorial to Wilfred Owen

Gayton

Thornton Hough

Parkgate Raby

M53 Bromborough

Raby Mere

Eastham

B5151

THE POETS' BENCH
NEW BRIGHTON

A memorial bench for literary contemplation overlooking the River Mersey, docks and Irish Sea.

Street Address: Kings Parade, New Brighton (A554)
Post Code: 86 / CH45 2PB - GPS: 53.436920, -3.067567

New Brighton Promenade is two miles long and, apparently, the longest promenade in England. The Poets' Bench is between exits Promenade 62 and 63 - the numbers are painted on ground by the steps down to the beach.

Lucy London, who began researching the First World War for a series of commemorative exhibitions in 2012, received a donation from a benefactor in America.   Following the closure of the Wilfred Owen Story Museum in Argyle Street, Birkenhead, Wirral, Lucy decided to have a First World War Wirral Poets Bench on King's Parade on the Promenade in New Brighton, Wirral, UK. The benches are organised by Wirral Older People's Parliament.

There were quite a few Wirral born or based First World War poets. With the help of Merseyside Historian Debbie Cameron and Liverpool Pals researcher Linda Woodfine Michelini, Lucy recently researched a Wallasey-born WW1 poet – Percy Haselden – who lived in New Brighton and taught art at Wallasey Grammar School.

The Wirral WW1 poets found so far and remembered on the Bench are:

1) Wilfred Owen (1893 – 1918) Born in Shropshire, lived in Birkenhead 1897 – 1907 and used to ride horses on New Brighton beach.

2 WW1 female poet May Sinclair (1863 – 1946) born Mary Amelia St. Clair on 24th August 1863 in Rock Ferry. May joined Dr. Hector Munro's Flying Ambulance Unit as Munro's Personal Assistant and travelled to Belgium with the Unit in September 1914, writing about her experiences on her return to Britain.

3) WW1 aviator poet Geoffrey Wall (1897 – 1917) born Arthur Geoffrey Nelson Wall in Liscard on 3rd March 1897. He lived in Denton Drive, New Brighton and was educated at Seabank Road High School. He joined the Royal Flying Corps in 1915 after going to live in Australia.

4) WW1 soldier poet Reginald Bancroft Cooke (1887 – 1946) born in Birkenhead in 1887. The family lived in Ashville Road, Claughton. He served in WW1 with the Princess Patricia's Canadian Light Infantry after going to live in America.

5) WW1 soldier poet Leonard Comer Wall (1896 – 1917) born in West Kirby, joined the West Lancashire Royal Field Artillery & was killed in June 1917. He left money for his horse Blackie to be repatriated. Blackie lived until 1942 and died at the age of 35 in the RSPCA facility in Hunts Cross, Liverpool - still bearing scars of the shrapnel that killed his master.

6) WW1 poet Olaf Stapledon (1886 – 1950) born in Egremont, as a conscientious objector he joined the Friends' Ambulance Unit

and served in France from July 1915 to January 1919. Awarded the French Croix de Guerre. He lived in Caldy – Stapledon Wood is named in his memory.

7) Percy Haselden (1886 – 1959) poet, teacher and artist. Born Percy Haselden Evans, Liscard. Lived in "End Cliff", Wellington Road, New Brighton in 1911. Art Master Wallasey Grammar School 1909 – 1920.

8) Celia, Lady Congreve (1867 – 1952) – British poet and WW1 nurse. Lived Burton Hall, Burton, nr Neston. Served Belgium & France; awarded Croix de Guerre, Reconnaissance Française & Belgian Medaille de la Reine Elisabeth for bravery for being one of the last nurses to leave Antwerp with the wounded in 1914. French Croix de Guerre for her bravery as a nurse at Rosières-aux-Salines, near Nancy, France. The hospital was shelled and bombed by aircraft in 1918.

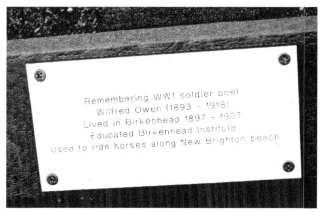

 Follow on Facebook:
The Poets' Bench New Brighton

Printed in Great Britain
by Amazon

23656169R00076